MY LIFE'S JOURNEY

FATHER PETER G. YOUNG

My Life's Journey

Peter G. Young

Copyright © 2022 by the Peter G. Young Foundation
134 Franklin Street
Albany, NY 12202

All rights reserved. No part of this book may be reproduced or transmitted in any form or by any means, electronic or mechanical, including photographing, recording, or by any information storage and retrieval system, without permission from the publisher, the Peter G. Young Foundation.

Peter G. Young Foundation, Inc.

ISBN: 979-8-218-01850-4

Printed in the United States of America

ABOUT THE AUTHOR

He was a ballplayer. A Navy veteran. A teacher. A human rights advocate. A Catholic priest. And a community activist. Father Peter G. Young left an indelible mark on New York's Capital Region, with his tireless dedication to helping some of society's most downtrodden citizens. His impact reached all across New York.

Before his passing in December 2020, Father Young had devoted over 50 years of his life in service to the community and the Catholic Church. He was ordained a Catholic priest in 1959 and eventually named pastor of St. John's Church in the South End of Albany, where he became known as a "street priest." In a church of loyal parishioners surrounded by drug dealing, gambling, prostitution and poverty, he learned firsthand how crime and addiction could destroy families and lives.

In 1985, Father Young founded Peter Young Housing, Industries and Treatment (PYHIT), which would grow into a statewide network of services that helped thousands of disenfranchised people regain their dignity. The homeless, people struggling with addiction, forgotten veterans, men and women involved in the criminal justice system…these are the people who found an ally in Father Young. PYHIT gave them treatment for their addiction, shelter, job training and a pathway back to a productive life.

From his student days at Christian Brothers Academy and Siena College, to his travels with the Negro Baseball League, to a stint with the U.S. Navy during the Korean War, and finally as a teacher at Cardinal McCloskey High School and upstart urban priest, Father Young was always a force of nature. He was especially proud of his lobbying efforts that led to the decriminalization of alcoholism in New York State.

"Father Pete" had a penchant for always leaving things better than he found them. Clearly, he has left all of us in a better place. And with the publishing of this book he leaves us one last thing: his story.

INTRODUCTION

"My Life's Journey" is the autobiography of Father Peter G. Young. Father Young devoted his entire life to developing programs, offering hope and assisting thousands of individuals through their own journey of addiction, recovery and living a productive life afterwards.

After ordination into the Catholic priesthood in 1959, Father Young was assigned to St. John's Parish located in the South End of Albany. His parishioners were a blend of immigrants—Italians, Irish, and African Americans. Some were poor and many suffered from addiction, mostly alcohol, in the late 1950s.

My Life's Journey is Father Young's own story of how he convinced local, state and federal government officials that alcoholism and later drug addiction were diseases, not crimes. His mission advocated a program of medical and psychological treatment, housing and a job. Not incarceration.

Father Young really never left his St. John's parishioners. He just expanded his parish to include many locations across New York State, from Brooklyn to Buffalo. In his role as Chaplain of the New York State Legislature, he learned that almost everybody has a spouse, relative or co-worker who suffers from some form of addiction. A good part of Father's journey was offering a helping hand to people on the road to recovery. In his role with the state Department of

Corrections, Father Young learned that most people in prison also suffered from some form of addiction. Same problem with the same solution—recognition and treatment, housing and the dignity of a job. This was Father Young's three-legged stool description of his programs.

Father Young wrote his autobiography during the last three years of his life. The effort slowed during his last six months as he battled a myeloma cancer which ended his journey December 9, 2020. His manuscript was gifted to the Peter G. Young Foundation, along with all of his other possessions. His supporters took up the tasks required to publish this book.

His close friends organized and edited his manuscript and wrote this introduction. The epilogue was also written by others followed by a description of the Peter G. Young entities that still operate today—all with the mission of continuing the legacy and programs implemented over the lifetime of Father Peter G. Young.

FOREWORD

For several years, countless friends encouraged me to write about my inner-city ministry and why it was sometimes considered controversial. Now, I am humbled to reflect upon the joy of ministry I have been privileged to share with so many of the forgotten in our society—especially the poor, the homeless, the alcohol and drug addicted and the incarcerated.

My journey spans 90 years of memories that I share with you here. It has surely been a ministry rooted in the Beatitudes. Many of the people I encountered over the years were "poor in spirit" but humble. They realized the gifts and blessings that come from a higher power. Those who humble themselves are able to accept their frail nature, to ask for forgiveness and to allow the grace of God to lead them to change.

I thank all of you who have assisted me in any way to bring about all of the significant changes that have so improved the lives of many of our brothers and sisters in need. God bless you and keep you safe.

Father Peter G. Young
Summer 2020

The Beatitudes

Blessed are the poor in spirit,
for theirs is the kingdom of heaven.
Blessed are they who mourn.
for they will be comforted.
Blessed are the meek,
for they will inherit the land.
Blessed are they who hunger and thirst for righteousness,
for they will be satisfied.
Blessed are the merciful,
for they will be shown mercy.
Blessed are the clean in heart,
for they will see God.
Blessed are the peacemakers,
for they will be called children of God.
Blessed are they who are persecuted for the
sake of righteousness,
for theirs is the Kingdom of Heaven.

Matthew 5:1-10

PART I

The Early Years

Life, Education, Preparation for Decision

I was born in Albany, New York, in 1930, a "Herbert Hoover Baby." My parents married during The Great Depression, when more than a quarter of the United States workforce was unemployed. My father was working at the Piping Rock Casino in Saratoga Springs, New York, and mother had just completed Mildred Elley Business School in Albany.

Having a baby to support during such tough economic times must have been a daunting challenge for my parents. Being an only child, babysitting was often a complex problem that required creative solutions. My mother was involved with many community and political groups, and my father was regarded as the best bowler in Albany, bowling at a different location almost every night. So, I was a "latchkey kid." Extended family members and friends kept an eye on me; they called me "Junior." My paternal grandparents lived nearby on First Street and would come to our house every day to check in on me, prepare food, clean the house and do laundry.

I grew up on Grove Avenue, in the New Scotland Avenue neighborhood of Albany. What a delight it was growing up in that part of town! Within one block of where I lived, there were over 100 kids. We were all friends, and it was easy to organize play activities without any adult leadership. We put together carnivals, camped out in empty lots and played pick-up baseball, football and basketball.

I was blessed to experience a middle-class education, always having fun with my friends while attending St. Teresa of Avila grammar school and later on high school at Christian Brothers Academy, both in Albany. In those days, so many grammar and high school students were registered in the Catholic school system. For me, life revolved around St. Teresa's Parish and Catholic Youth Organization activities. Those became part of my routine, and venues for bonding in the glory days of the 1940s after World War II.

During the war, dad went to work making tanks in Schenectady, New York. My mother worked for the state until she retired with great health at just 55 years old. She always said, "This is great. I'm retired and I still get a check every month." Both she and my dad lived until the age of 87.

Since mom and dad both worked every day, I joined every activity and sports team I could find at Christian Brothers Academy to stay busy. Then I'd walk home for our 6pm dinner. Our neighbors supervised me, and poor behavior would be reported to my parents if things did not go well while they were at work. The school and the neighborhood knew my every move.

For me, growing up in Albany was a delightful experience. In those days, the concept of "It Takes a Village" really worked. While in grammar school, I saw a note on a community bulletin board that said baseball instruction was available from one Art Mitchell. Art was an outstanding teacher who had enjoyed a great career in the National Negro League before moving to Albany. He would become an influential mentor to me during this period.

Without telling my parents, I rode my bicycle to nearby Lincoln

Park, where I was the only one to show up that day for Art's baseball school. Although I didn't realize it at the time, it was a turning point in my life. I got to know and love the Black community, which provided me with a foundation for over 70 years of a uniquely rewarding life and ministry.

Art taught me the fundamentals of baseball and became one of my most important role models. I would travel with his Black Sox as the only white person and witness the team experience insults and discrimination. On Saturdays, he would put me through drills that helped me develop the skills I would need to make the starting lineup as a freshman on the varsity baseball team at Christian Brothers Academy.

Later, Art became a leader in the civil rights movement and developed a network of vital community programs in the Albany area. I admired his style and ability to unify angry, headstrong religious leaders. Exposure to Art's world prepared me well for the many racist and discriminatory acts I would witness and experience. It was years before Rosa Parks would refuse to give up her seat on a bus to a white man, a watershed moment in the civil rights movement. I could not have foreseen how difficult the days ahead would be, or how these struggles would change the trajectory of my ministry.

At CBA, Brother Victor Dardis, FSC, helped me develop the skills and confidence I would need to navigate through my teenage years. He was an extraordinary religious brother and also the athletic director at the school. He was another early mentor for me and kept me on the straight-and-narrow as a student in both academics and athletics. Recognizing my interest in baseball, he sent me to see the varsity coach. Up to bat for the first time as a freshman, I hit a home run.

I became CBA's first baseman for the next four years. The confidence Brother Victor had in me helped me secure an athletic scholarship at Siena College in Loudonville, New York, where I would continue my education. I felt deeply indebted to him. When I was ordained years later, my first Mass was to honor Brother Victor, who by then was teaching at Manhattan College in New York City. I wanted to thank him for believing in me and guiding me.

Looking back at those days, I remember thinking about what I could do to help people in need and others by becoming an independent thinker and innovator. I was never distracted by the desire to have a drink or try smoking—largely because Brother Victor told me it would diminish my motivation to be a good athlete. I had my first glass of wine and beer at age 35 and had not yet tried smoking!

Mom and dad were firm believers that at 18, I should be on my own financially and pay my own way. This led me to take on a number of interesting jobs during my teens. My aunt got me my first paying job at age 14, working in the mailroom of what is now the Alfred E. Smith State Office Building in Albany. One of my duties was to collect mysterious little envelopes from employees throughout the building and take them down to a news kiosk in the lobby. Sometimes, the person who ran the kiosk would hand me envelopes to bring back to particular people. I didn't figure out what was going on until one of the women receiving an envelope scored a big win and gave me a tip. I realized then that I was part of a "numbers game" played right in the state office building, with me as the delivery boy.

After graduating from CBA, I decided to pursue a degree in business and finance at Siena College. Most of my classmates from high school were also going to Siena. Although I was offered an athletic scholarship and academic opportunities out of town, I wanted to remain close to my girlfriend in Albany.

Mom and dad felt it was my decision: work or college. When I chose college, they left it up to me, at age 18, to find the resources to attend Siena. Somehow, I summoned the nerve to approach the athletic director at Siena, Father Maurice Fitzgerald. I told him that I was eager to attend the school, but needed a scholarship to do so. I knew Siena was looking for talent, so I told Father Fitzgerald I had been an All-Albany baseball player. We made a deal: I would work for the athletic department and he would enroll me. I still can't get over how much nerve it took to do that, and without anyone telling me how or backing me up. It taught me that if you really want something, you must have the courage to ask for help!

Playing for Siena during my freshman year, I was injured in a game against Cornell and confined to a wheelchair for several months. I ended up with an "interesting" roommate at the hospital—a fellow who would sneak out of our room at 11pm, scamper down the fire escape, and visit the local bar. What's more, his wife would bring him a vase of flowers accompanied by a bottle of Scotch. He would still be drunk at 10am when the doctor made rounds. Asked how he felt, the guy would reply, "Tired, doc." It was a Workers' Compensation case and a learning experience that helped me understand addiction.

My baseball scholarship lasted three years. In 1952, the Middle Atlantic College leadership said Siena was granting too many athletic scholarships. Consequently, even though I was team captain, my scholarship was eliminated for that year. In order to continue receiving financial assistance, I was assigned to do all of the laundry for the *entire* athletic department. I ran loads through 28 Maytag washing machines several times a day. I had to make certain no soap was left on the uniforms that might cause irritation. Coach Dan Cunha would watch me relentlessly and check my work. Players on the basketball team and other friends gave me the nickname "Wet Wash."

Happily, I was also promoted to director of ticket sales for home basketball games. It was great! I became a very popular guy on campus among people in pursuit of tickets. Our basketball team ranked in the top 20 in the nation. After beating Seton Hall with driving layups by Tom Pottenburg and Billy Harrell to close out the game, we moved up to 11th in the Associated Press national standings. All of the athletic scholarship students lived together on campus, an experience that strengthened our bonds of friendship. We continued to meet several times a year after graduation to rehash old times.

While in college, I also joined the summer travel team of former Major League baseball star Nick Iarossi. I learned to play the game better, and it was fun traveling to state fairs. Nick had worked out a way to ensure we would always get paid. Around the fifth inning of the first game, he would call out someone in the stands and start a fight. The fracas pulled in a larger crowd, and our team would get the second-game gate money, jump in our cars and drive out of town—quickly!

Sports gave me confidence and kept me extremely motivated in school. Everyone needs to experience success. Later, while teaching at Cardinal McCloskey High School in Albany and working in addiction-recovery programs, I would encourage people to extend themselves and find ways to be creative. We all need to embrace the challenges of a very competitive society.

My dating experiences during high school and college were mostly a series of blunders. All of the cadets at CBA wore dress white uniforms to the senior prom, including me. My date was Marilyn Yanas. The day of the prom, I had been boxing with the New York State YMCA team. Unfortunately, I had taken a few too many shots to the nose. That evening, as my date and I danced in the CBA gym, a nosebleed quietly covered my date and me with streams of red. Even against our pressed whites, the blood went unnoticed thanks to a ruby glow that filled the room—a lighting scheme inspired by our prom theme. After our dance, Marilyn went to the powder room. It was then that I heard the scream, followed by: "Let's get out of here… we're both covered with blood!"

Obviously, proms were not my thing. I was more of a "canteen" type, often hanging out at the Lion's Den at Vincentian Institute in Albany, or at the CYO center for meet-and-greet dances. Afterward, we would walk the girls home, frequently stopping for ice cream.

One night, my date ordered an ice cream sundae. Checking my pocket to see what remained of my allowance, and noting the cost of a sundae, I calculated that I could get one as well. So we ordered. Then she saw the Pepsi sign, and I knew I was in trouble. While she enjoyed her ice cream and soda, I shared my predicament with the owner. He was less than sympathetic, grabbing my ice cream and telling me to leave the store. That was my last date with this particular young lady.

Then there was the College of Saint Rose prom with Ellen Morrissey. Ellen was an amazing woman and co-chair of the event. I knew that I was competing with my friend Howie Nolan for her affection. So I dutifully ordered her a corsage, but unwittingly asked the florist to deliver it the day *after* the prom. As part of her role as co-chair, Ellen stood at the entrance to the event to greet the guests as they arrived. When I came along, she slugged me in my mid-section and asked, "Where are my flowers?"

Seeing a Need, a Turning Point and a Difficult Decision

In 1948, with the Korean conflict grabbing headlines, I decided to join the Naval Reserve Unit in Albany. My hope was to attend the St.

Louis Cardinals baseball training camp after graduating from Siena in 1952. Instead, as fate would have it, I received a letter to report for active duty in the U.S. Navy immediately after graduation.

My experience in the Navy was an awakening to a bigger world. I loved my time in the service, with the exception of basic training. Our integrated Albany unit was the first with Black shipmates to be assigned to a southern base. This resulted in many fights amongst the men. We experienced firsthand the racial differences embedded in southern culture.

Prior to the Navy, my only real experience traveling had been on road trips with athletic teams. When I reported to the Brooklyn Navy Yard, I was assigned to an auxiliary minesweeper, the smallest round-bottomed ship in the fleet. I quickly learned what being seasick was all about. On one mission, our captain got drunk and we grounded the boat on a sandbar. The mistake forced us to spend many cold days and nights aboard our vessel near Bay City, Michigan, while repairs were made.

Once on active duty, I was transferred to a variety of ships, including a destroyer escort similar to the USS Slater docked at the Port of Albany. Our ship cruised the Atlantic coast on patrol. This was not a bad assignment since it was during the Korean conflict, and I didn't need to worry about enemies shooting at me.

A turning point in my life came while we toured islands in the Caribbean and along the East Coast. The ship would routinely pull into ports for supplies and fuel. While ashore, many of our crew would make unwelcome, forceful sexual advances on local women. I found this behavior contemptible. At 267 pounds and in great shape, I had no fear or reservations about intervening. I took on the volunteer role of "shore patrol" and tried to put a stop to their mistreatment of local women. The values I had learned from my family and through my education told me that women were to be respected. Physical confrontations with shipmates who did not share these values usually ended in my favor, albeit with some minor battle scars.

One night while on watch duty, the captain noticed that I was bleeding and asked what had happened. I told him I had been in a fight on shore with two of the guys after they had drank too much and then sexually assaulted some native women. The captain said, "Young, have you ever considered becoming a chaplain?" He told me I could truly make a difference as a young sailor if I took his advice. "Chaplains get the respect needed to accomplish what you're trying to do with these men."

From that day forth, the captain often repeated his suggestion that I become a chaplain. One night while standing watch on the forward bulkhead, seawater splashing in my face every time the bow dipped below a wave, I reflected on his urging. This might indeed be an opportunity for me to continue my education and become an "agent of change." However, such a decision would involve other people in my life.

The most significant person for me during college and my time in the Navy was Eileen Cox. I was in love with Eileen. She was a respected nurse and at the time was taking graduate school classes in New York City. The letters I received from Eileen while away led me to think of the days ahead and how we couldn't wait to see each other. She was remarkable, and I was the luckiest guy in the world to be with her.

I tossed and turned at night over how to tell her about my desire to accept the captain's challenge and pursue a path to the ministry. I thought about it for many months while at sea. Eileen and I had been dating for two years. How could I tell her of my decision to consider the priesthood?

At the conclusion of our cruise, the captain accompanied me to the administration building at the Brooklyn Navy Yard to tell them that I wanted to attend chaplain's school. It was the end of the Korean War, and obtaining permission to sign out of the service was fairly easy, especially with my captain preparing the necessary paperwork. As I stood there about to resign from active duty in favor of chaplain's school, I thought about recent letters from Eileen. Her writing described our plans to go with her family on vacation to Lake George when I got home. It made my decision all the more difficult.

When I finally did get home, my friend Howie Nolan called right away. He invited Eileen and I to join him and his date for a day at the Saratoga Race Course. We decided to go, and in the car on the way home Eileen and I sat close together in the back seat. I quietly told her that I wanted to try the seminary. I explained how the captain had promised me that I would be able to help so many people by going into ministry. Eileen listened, and did not say a word. When Howie later asked why we were so quiet during the car ride home, I told him I was going into the seminary. He was amazed.

Soon, my decision would surprise many others as well. My intentions to pursue marriage were changing, but not without great reservation. I was trying to justify leaving such a wonderful person as Eileen Cox for the unknown of becoming a priest. Only a strong desire to help others kept me focused on the seminary, but I spent many sleepless nights wondering if it was the right decision. I knew Eileen would be a wonderful partner in life. I thought how great it would be to raise a big family with her. However, the opportunity to help others as a chaplain challenged me to try it.

Howie shared my change in plans with his college classmate Fred Martin, who later became a respected attorney in Westchester County. Fred wasted no time pursuing Eileen. They eventually married and had many great, talented children. I visited with Fred and Eileen often. The last time I saw her was in a New York City hospital, where I prayed with her before she passed away. Later, I had the joy and privilege of being the priest to witness the marriage of some of their children. I still keep in touch with her family.

I was lucky to experience a very normal social life before heading to the seminary—to feel the ups and downs of dating when growing up. Many of my fellow seminarians were products of a strict religious formation right through college.

Road to the Priesthood and Ordination

Although I had attended Mass regularly, I was never an altar boy. Nor did I participate in any church-related activities other than the CYO. I was just an average guy who was very persistent when it came to goals I believed in. Now, I wanted to give the priesthood a try and become a chaplain. But there were so many people applying for the seminary at the time, it was very difficult to get in. (How times have changed!)

My road to the priesthood became problematic. In 1953, I went to the Albany Diocesan Chancery and was told that I did not have the necessary background to enter under their admission policies. My degree in finance and administration from Siena did not satisfy their requirements. They told me a major or a minor in philosophy and language studies was necessary preparation for the seminary.

Not knowing what to do, I met with a family friend, Father Joseph Varden, an experienced and well-respected priest. He agreed to advocate for my acceptance as a diocesan candidate. We went to the chancery together and Father Varden asked, "What must Peter do to prove that he's sincere about his vocation? Can he go to a seminary preparation program?" The chancellor said, "That's up to him, but as a diocese, we're not making any commitment. He'll have to find a way to cover his own academic costs."

That gave me a green light to at least give it a try. I went shopping for a seminary prep program and found that the least expensive one in the U.S. cost about $3,000 a year. Father Varden suggested I call some of his contacts, who recommended that I research programs in Canada.

I was directed to St. Jerome's Seminary, which operated under the authority of Ottawa University. They offered all of the programs in classical languages and philosophy that the diocese insisted I complete before reapplying. St. Jerome's room, board and tuition totaled only $670 a year U.S. with the Canadian exchange rate. What a deal! I quickly packed my bags and headed north. I still feel like I owe St. Jerome's more money when I hear the cost of a current college education.

I worked at a country club in Albany during the summers. Starting at 6am, I would whisk down the greens to push the dew back into the ground. At 9am, I rolled the clay tennis courts. When that was done, I reported to the pool for lifeguard duty at 11am. Finally, in the late afternoon and evening, I went to the dining room to wait tables and then bartended until midnight, earning 50 cents an hour.

The valedictorian of my Siena graduating class worked alongside me at the club bar, which turned out to be a problem. Club management told me he was "conspicuously Italian" and some of the members had difficulty with him being there. I knew that he needed money, so I asked if he could work in the kitchen, in the "back of the house." It was one of those sad episodes of discrimination that all too often go forgotten.

Working at the country club was always about logging as many paid hours as I could. The members treated me well and I got to play golf for free. It also gave me an opportunity to network my way into a side job: catering home parties for the members. I needed the extra money and became friendly with many local business and community leaders. Several offered me jobs and opportunities for growth. The CEO of Blue Cross/Blue Shield promised me employment. Another one of my favorite members, Jim Haggerty, was President Dwight Eisenhower's special assistant and press director. Jim would pass along all of the news from Washington while I waited on him.

Two nights a week I would sneak off to play first base for the Roxy team in the Twilight League. This offered me an opportunity to keep up my interest in baseball.

Life back at St. Jerome's settled into a very confining routine. Obedience to the rules was a priority. I enjoyed living in a community of men, as I had in college and the Navy. That part was much the same at St. Jerome's, but their rules were always testing us for humility and obedience. At the time, I did not appreciate them. It was a long and difficult journey from my captain's words of encouragement to my ordination day.

There were about 150 students at St. Jerome's. We received lots of personal attention. Some of the guys had come directly from high school, others from college and still others from careers already in progress. We lived in an overcrowded dorm in a fourth-floor walkup, and we did so without a complaint. The food was terrible, so we would go to the Ottawa Amish Market and stock up on survival supplies: lots of cheese and bread for the week.

The only opportunity for physical recreation was hockey. I had never played hockey in the States, but it was a part of the daily routine in Canada. Our schedule required us to get out of the building for one period each day, and hockey was the only activity available in the colder weather. We all became interested in ice skating. One of the students in our class was a star in the Ice Capades; he gave us all instruction on how to skate. I gravitated toward playing goalie because I was awkward and built low to the ground. Also, my baseball background helped me quickly adapt to catching a puck using the goalie's glove.

We had little more than the bare basics, but our diverse personalities enabled us to pull together and create our own fun. Overall, Canada was a great experience. I am forever grateful to our northern neighbors for providing me with an affordable way to prepare for the seminary.

I completed my pre-seminary studies at St. Jerome's and earned my degree at Ottawa University. The Albany Diocese told me that if I wanted to register for the seminary under their sponsorship, I would need six more years of training. I was assigned to Christ the King Seminary in Olean, just five miles north of the Pennsylvania border in the most western part of New York State. The routine was consistent: chapel, study and classes, with no variation. We all bonded with our classmates and became good friends.

The instructors, mostly Franciscans, based their style of education on the thinking of St. Francis. It was a lot different from the Jesuits I had studied with in Canada. The Franciscan emphasis was aimed at preparing us for a life of humility and service to the church. Academics were naturally a part of the program, but the friars were always demonstrating by their words and actions how those committed to ministry had to be in the servant model.

The Holy Spirit works in interesting ways. A seminary friend and deacon once left a copy of Time magazine in my room, a violation of the rule against possessing secular reading material. I was put on probation and forced to return to Albany to meet with Bishop William

Scully, hopefully to obtain permission to return to the seminary. I had to hitch a ride back to attend the meeting, where a promise of obedience to the rules would hopefully win the Bishop's approval. All of this discipline was difficult for me. It was different for some of the younger guys, who were accustomed to that type of control. My previous college and private life had been much more relaxed. Adjusting to this regimentation was challenging for me. However, I was allowed to return to the seminary in Olean.

I thought of myself as being in the bottom half of our class. I'm only guessing about that, because the faculty at Christ the King Seminary never posted any scores or exam results. That said, we knew when things did not work out for one of our classmates. We might be in chapel when someone was unceremoniously driven to the bus stop, and we would notice an empty seat. Eventually, we would learn that the dean had arranged for that student to continue his education elsewhere.

I was always amazed how bright my peers were. In high school, at CBA, I failed my French II exam and was astonished by the language skills of my classmates. Still, I've always been grateful for the academic foundation CBA afforded me.

At the seminary, I admired the other students' ability to quickly comprehend assignments, especially since most classes were in Latin, and languages were not my strong suit. But it also made me feel dumb.

I've always pressured myself to be my best at any task. My habit of putting too many irons in the fire was a major problem during my college days. Multitasking has been both an asset and a liability my whole life. In college, working two jobs and pursuing athletics always resulted in me not doing anything well. Even in the seminary, my studies were usually a last-minute cram to absorb the required information. Looking back on it now, at age 90, I see how the Holy

Spirit was guiding me toward a ministry where multiple people and problems would demand my attention daily.

Back at Christ the King Seminary, at the time a part of St. Bonaventure College, our rector was Father Thomas Plassman, a six-foot-four, 70-plus-year-old German and true scholar. His age never stopped him from going out every day for two hours to complete his chores. He took good care of the grounds, and it was not beneath him to scrub and mop the floors. He was nationally known for his books and research, but always down-to-earth.

Father Plassman once took note of some partially completed brickwork for a new addition to the seminary. He called over the contractor and said, "Take it down. I don't want smooth brick; I want rough brick, to symbolize the type of candidates we're preparing for the ministry."

"Priestly men and manly priests," he always said. The ministry needed men who would be willing to accept difficult assignments. The building was filled with symbols of what we were expected to be. Now, it's a women's dorm.

During my last year at the seminary, Father Plassman said he would be doubling our classes. As it was, we only had an hour of free time daily, and now we had to give that up. Nevertheless, it was what Father Plassman wanted, and we knew about his dedication. He expected the same from us. When he completed the coursework, he told us that he had terminal cancer. Within a month, he went on to God for his reward. Siena College has a building named in his honor.

My ordination took place at the Cathedral of the Immaculate Conception in Albany on Saturday, May 23, 1959. Bishop William Scully was the presiding bishop. On that day, he imposed hands on 11 new priests.

My first Mass was celebrated at my home parish, St. Teresa of Avila on New Scotland Avenue in Albany. Father John Hart was the pastor, a man who could be gruff and blunt. I was nervous offering that first Latin Mass, and I guess my voice hinted at my uneasiness—especially my singing voice. Father Hart offered some remarks at the end of the Mass: "Well, what do you know, Peter Young is a priest, and we just heard him shout at God for one hour!" My mother was taken aback and anything but pleased by his humor, but I've never been able to carry a tune, so I knew he was right.

My dad opposed my decision to enter the priesthood because he wanted me to raise a family. His was so very different from my mom's Irish family. Dad came from a long line of German Lutheran ancestors, and I was the only male left to carry on the Young name. They had been well off and very successful for a century until 1888, when they went broke due to the Civil War. He felt pressured to continue that heritage through me, and from the day I entered the seminary, he did not speak to me, hoping to somehow change my mind.

There were many difficult years of sitting at the table or being in the house without a word from him. Two years after I was ordained, dad had an opportunity to witness my happiness in the priesthood. We had a talk and I told him that it was my decision. He then became my biggest supporter, volunteering for a number of causes in the Parish Church.

Mom was a first-generation immigrant from Ireland. Her parents came to America as children. Dad's family always looked down on her Irish roots. That never worried her, but still his family put forth an air of superiority. Nonetheless, mom and dad had a successful marriage with lots of love and steady work habits. Dad was the silent one and Mom was always networking.

I began my ministry at St. John's the Baptist Church on Green Street in Albany. It was the good work of Father Jim Hart, Vicar General of the Diocese of Albany, that sent me to this neighborhood in the city's South End. The day before our ordination, our class was called to the chancery. We each waited for our turn to meet with Bishop William Scully and find out where we would be sent for ministry. Before I was called in, the bishop received a note from Father Hart bearing specific instructions. And with that, I was assigned to report to St. John the Baptist Church.

My First Assignment – St. John the Baptist Church

Unlike most classes, we were not given a break between our ordination and reporting to our first assignment. My last night at home, I loaded all of my clothing and ordination gifts into my new car. I wanted to be ready to leave first thing in the morning. About 3:00am, a crash outside of our house woke me from a sound sleep. A drunk driver had totaled my car. Plan B: transfer all of my belongings to my dad's car and be on my way.

I pulled up in front of St. John's Rectory on May 25, 1959, and went looking for the pastor, Father George McKeon. Before I could finish climbing the steps to the front door, a woman approached me saying she needed help. Being newly ordained, I mustered my sense of commitment and asked her how I could assist. She said she needed a ride to Social Services to pick up her check.

It sounded simple enough. I knew the office was nearby in City Hall on the ground floor, so I decided to give her a lift. She was smoking a cigarette as we drove, thankfully flicking the butt out of the partly rolled-down window of dad's car when we arrived at our destination.

I could sense this was not going to be a pleasant exchange when the woman demanded her check from the clerk at Social Services. "You've been told this before," said the clerk, "why are you back here drunk again?" The woman promptly punched the clerk in the left side of the face, knocking her right off her chair! As a security guard approached, my charge ran into the ladies room and locked herself in a stall. "You brought her in Father," said the guard, "you get her out!" I tried, but she refused to budge. The situation was getting more difficult with each passing moment.

Suddenly, I heard sirens and fully expected this episode would end in a police action. While the woman and I exchanged shouts through the stall door, a firefighter tapped me on the shoulder. "Father, do you own the Pontiac parked outside?"

"Yes," I responded.

"Father, I hate to tell you this, but your car just went up in flames!" Apparently, the woman's attempt to throw the butt out the window missed, and it bounced off the glass and into the back seat where my belongings and unopened ordination gifts were now smoldering.

I called a friend, Jim Powers, to help me secure my third car on that very first day of ministry. I hadn't even stepped into the rectory yet!

St. John's Church was located in one of the more depressed parts of Albany, a small tract in the South End dubbed the "Red Light District" by city police. It was an area where prostitution, drug dealing and alcohol abuse occurred unchecked by police, facilitated by a warped brand of bureaucratic reasoning: confine such illicit activities to this one neighborhood, and the rest of the city would remain relatively free of them. Reporters described the neighborhood around St. John's as a "crime containment area." It included Green Street, Dongan Avenue, South Ferry Street and from Hamilton to

Church streets and one block west to Plum Street.

I wanted to learn more about the area around St. John's Parish, where I would be living and working, so I confronted local political leaders. They admitted that they were aware of the high crime level. The police and politicians knew every drug dealer, gambling operation and house of prostitution. The police protected their informants, their "eyes and ears" in the neighborhood. Their philosophy was to monitor and control these unsavory elements in order to prevent them from spreading. Most of these criminal activities were also tolerated by the community and the code and zoning staff. It was amazing how they were accepted and allowed to operate.

For most of my ministry at St John's, I would live without worry for my safety. With their trusted snitches, the locals in charge knew the comings and goings of all visitors, especially criminal competitors trying to bust into the turf and take away business. Somehow these newcomers could never meet city safety codes.

I would make my home and ministry within these boundaries for the next 18 years. For much of it, I would resent the negative reporting about the area by local papers and other media. I came to know the majority of "South-Enders" as good neighbors who were ethical and proud of their community.

Long before crime and prostitution became the norm, the St. John's neighborhood had been a center for Irish immigrants. When the "shanty wave" arrived in America—a group looked down upon in their homeland—they were not well received at nearby St. Mary's Parish. They were also resented by the well-to-do "lace curtain" Irish who preceded them. On Sundays, the shanty wave folks were relegated to the balcony pews at St. Mary's.

In 1815, a small group of the new immigrants purchased an old church from the Dutch Reformed congregation on South Ferry

Street and established their own parish. Initially, the Albany Diocese would not register it. For many years, the founders of what would become St. John's hired their own clergy without the authority of church leaders until the diocese finally agreed to recognize them. All of their clergy did amazing work and were committed to serving whoever appeared at the front door. Much later, Monsignor Reilly, a former pastor at St. John's, and I wrote an 80-page account of their remarkable story.

In his book *The Catholic Church in New York*, the Rev. John Talbot Smith claims that a second Catholic Church existed in Albany in 1830. A non-Catholic historian insists that the congregation of St. John's occupied three different buildings before the present edifice was put into service. We know of two for certain: They used a building on the corner of Herkimer and Franklin streets from 1837 to 1839, and the present school building on the corner of Ferry and Dallius streets. Perhaps as early as 1815, or even earlier, Mass was celebrated in a mission chapel in the South End for the convenience of families living there. Priests of St. Mary's Church attended this chapel.

Over time, the Catholic population in the South Ferry neighborhood grew so large that people decided to establish an independent parish. It appears this move was bitterly opposed by the Trustees of St. Mary's. There are veiled references to deceit, double-dealing and contention among the parishes concerned. It seems that Fr. Gregory Pardou, curate at St. Mary's under Rev. Charles Smith, was ministering to the people of the South End and was either commissioned by his superiors or took it upon himself to sound out people's sentiment concerning the founding a separate parish. A parish was needed, the people wanted it, and as a result, St. John's was organized early in 1837.

In the meantime, Fr. Smith was transferred from St. Mary's and

Fr. Pardou was appointed to succeed him. The trustees, however, were so displeased with Fr. Pardou and his interest in the people of the South End that they petitioned the bishop to have him removed. In an effort to keep the peace, Fr. Pardou was sent to take charge of the newly organized parish and was actually the first pastor of St. John's, although that honor is generally ascribed to Rev. John Kelly. Fr. Kelly succeeded Fr. Pardou who, after only a few months as pastor, became ill and returned to New York where he passed to his final reward in 1838.

A peek into the files of the *Albany Argus* for the year 1837 provides a few interesting sidelights about the city in the year St. John's was established. The Right Reverend John Dubois was at that time bishop of the Diocese of New York, which included Albany. The governor was the Hon. W.L. Marcy, the Mayor of Albany was Erastus Corning I, and Andrew Jackson had just been re-elected to the U.S. presidency through the overwhelming support of common people, as opposed to the will of bankers and social elites.

The political situation was remarkably similar to that of today. The partisan bitterness that existed may be presumed from the following few quotes taken from the *Albany Evening Journal* of January 25, 1837: "The party (Democratic) has found another renegade priest to endorse General Jackson's religious character. The fellow's name is McCullom – he deserves the whipping post." Under the heading of shipping news: "The number of vessels visiting the Port of Albany during the past season was 380, from 32 foreign ports." A few days later, under local news: "A preliminary meeting was held and committees were formed to consider ways and means for proceeding with the foundation of the proposed Albany Medical College."

Such was the Albany of over 170 years ago. How little it differed from the city today.

The loyalty of the old-timers to St. John's Church was as strong and active during my ministry as it was in the hearts of their hardy forebears. Fr. Kelly managed to acquire the property for the sum of $15,500 and, with very little remodeling, the sturdy stone structure was rendered suitable for Catholic worship. It served the parishioners of St. John's for almost 70 years.

The purchase of the church property occurred in February 1839, but let us not overlook perhaps a more important event, which, according to the most reliable tradition, took place the previous year: the founding of St. John's Parish School. The first teachers were lay teachers from Ireland and the school continued under their supervision until 1852, when Bishop John McCloskey brought the Daughters of Charity to the diocese from their Motherhouse in Emmetsburg, Maryland.

The demographics of the neighborhood were always changing. During World War I and the years that followed, it became known as an Italian neighborhood. When I was assigned there in 1959, the parish was 95 percent white. Within just 10 years it was 95 percent Black. Mortgage redlining helped it become the highest crime area in upstate New York. However, all of St. John's records show the parish as having an outstanding spiritual and social service ministry.

Father McKeon and Daily Life at St. John's

The pastor of St. John's at the time, Father George McKeon, was a saintly man who exemplified the philosophy of charity. I have always tried to follow his admirable example. The day after I arrived, he returned from a medical examination in Boston and told me that his spinal cancer was progressing. He would need to turn administration of the parish over to me in its entirety.

Three priests had been transferred to other locations and Fr. McKeon, Fr. Herb, a mission priest, and I replaced them in May 1959. Fr. Herb was in residence at St. John's, but his responsibility was to offer weekend retreats and preach missions throughout the Northeast. This meant that I would need to take on full responsibility for church services, the school, the buildings, the cemetery, social service programs, the clothing center, the furniture bank, youth programs, the immigrant resource center, the parish hall, convent, rectory and the monstrous, Gothic-style building. Undertaking all of this was more than a challenge, because not only was I assigned to the parish, but also appointed to a full-time teaching position at Cardinal McCloskey High School a few blocks away (now Bishop Maginn High School).

The parish's average income was $350 a week from collections. We wrote to foundations for support and were rewarded and endorsed by Governor Nelson A. Rockefeller's administration. Our reputation on Green Street was well established, but our programs needed more media attention. With the help of the Kennedy and Johnson administrations and assistance from Congressmen Leo O'Brien and Sam Stratton, we were able to connect with leaders in Congress. My friendship with A. Philip Randolph, a well-known labor and civil rights activist, served us well in establishing vital new state programs.

To complicate my new assignment even more, I was replacing a curate who had a wonderful reputation and was totally committed to the community. Father Charles Damann was the person everyone depended upon for help with virtually every aspect of his or her life. I always admired his dedication to needy residents in the South End. He operated the best youth program in the city and had hundreds of youngsters playing in the gym and activity rooms every night. He would drive the parish furniture truck every day, and people didn't like the idea that I did not have the time to do that with my teaching schedule and other duties. The parishioners were quick to remind me that, "You aren't any Father Damann." He was amazing and did outstanding work for the church. It was all but impossible for anyone to replace him without falling short of expectations.

To make all the ministries of the parish possible, we pursued every state and federal program related to poverty that we could find. We secured enough money to support almost all of our programs with full-time staff within five years. It was easy to apply for the many new programs under the Johnson administration, and our local demographics proved that we were a high-poverty area.

The St. John's rectory was a huge, circa 1815 building. I found out rather quickly that we would have many "guests." Some priests who had been removed from their regular assignments came to our rectory while working on putting their lives back together. Father McKeon always welcomed priests who arrived with drinking or emotional problems. Most of them were good men living in rural communities where they had found too much time to become a friend of alcohol. As an old adage goes, "Man takes a drink, the drink takes a drink, and then the drink takes the man."

Father McKeon was a deeply spiritual man, and his hospitality helped inspire our troubled brothers to rebuild their own spirituality and restore meaning to their wounded spirits. It was his example, his support and his simple lifestyle that they admired. It was amazing to see how happy Father McKeon was in his ministry, even when in tremendous pain caused by his spinal cancer.

Father McKeon and I would take nightly walks along South Pearl Street because he wanted to show that there was a religious presence in the neighborhood. On warm summer nights, the stoops were full of families that we would meet and greet. Two blocks to the west, on Franklin and Green streets, you would encounter the negative elements that the city permitted without objection.

Many well-known jazz entertainers frequented Green Street, and the crowds that followed them supported us with words of encouragement whenever we visited to hear their concerns. We always suggested that they to come to our office for help with their problems.

We witnessed many fights with outsiders that were never reported to the police, and we tried to mediate our neighbors' differences. Local folks would try to calm them down saying, "Don't put your business in the street." The locals feared encounters with the police, especially one officer who would beat them up before taking them to the station house. The police avoided filing reports about anything that would result in unnecessary media attention.

One night, after closing the youth program, I left to accompany Father McKeon on one of our therapeutic walks. As usual, he was outside of the church waiting for me. But when I opened the door, I saw my slight, 118-pound pastor across the street being used as a human shield by a naked female prostitute. The woman was trying to avoid being punched by an unhappy customer, who was also without clothing.

Maria Lupian, our housekeeper, happened to see what was going on and quickly came to the rescue. With one swing of a baseball bat, she knocked the naked man to the ground while the prostitute retreated to the brothel. Maria was a fierce protector of the rectory and Fr. McKeon. Suffice it to say I could share many other stories to prove that point!

In 1959, our parish began operating a nightly shelter after the gym youth program closed, with over 100 homeless people coming in after 9pm to stay the night. I was gaining a more realistic understanding of the problem of alcohol addiction. The broken priests who lived with us were just as vulnerable as the drunks we housed on cots in the gym. I began to see proof that addiction does not discriminate.

When I came back to the rectory at night, I would often find one of our guest priests inebriated and continuing his addictive behavior. They had a variety of styles. One would fill a large container with ice, mix it with gin and vermouth, and sip from it all day. Another was an avid fan of Jack Daniels, and a third preferred beer. When I discovered one of them drinking quietly in his room, I would encourage them to go to Alcoholics Anonymous and sometimes escort them to an open meeting.

Diocesan officials called me about rumors that I had taken priests to AA meetings. I told the chancery staff that, in fact, I had taken them, to help them regain their dignity and move toward recovery. I was allowed to continue, but certain clergy leaders were not happy about it since public intoxication was still considered a crime in the 1950s and 1960s.

These addicted clergy provided us with many confusing—but funny—experiences. Father McKeon and I always volunteered to drive them when they went out, so they would stay out of trouble. Inevitably, some would end up at a nearby bar late at night. We would walk or drive around the neighborhood to track them down and return them to the rectory. The diocese insisted we control their behavior or send them to the bishop if they strayed.

All of this helped me see addiction as an illness. It became my mission to discover "why" certain people needed to drink. These priests were good people, but with an irresistible urge to drink. The same was true of the men and women in our shelter and hundreds more who came to our parish office. They were decent folks. but their brain told them they must satisfy their cravings—like some sort of disease.

Around 1959, I began working to become a professional in the field of addiction. I was determined to have the disease of alcoholism reclassified as an illness rather than a crime. It became an all-consuming agenda for my life. After 14 years and some 30,000 meetings, we would succeed in getting the law changed: alcoholism was designated a chronic disease in the nation's legal and medical vernacular.

In the early days, my priority was caring for people who were nightly problem guests in our network of shelters and getting them medical care. The work of numerous volunteer fellowship staff in local emergency rooms helped defuse any disputes and get these people where they needed to be quickly.

Father McKeon used a different tactic for our clergy. He would confine the inebriated soul to his room to sleep off the effects of his drinking under a watchful eye. When the problem priest sobered up, he would receive a lecture about what God expected of him. This nightly routine was exhausting, and for me compounded by my obligation to say the 7am Mass and quickly head off to my high school teaching assignments.

There were no New York State-sponsored treatment programs for alcoholics back then. Most of the struggling clergy were able to regain their dignity in recovery and return to ministry after a short stay and some help from AA friends.

A federal program attempted to do research on people treated at their site in Lexington, Kentucky. All of the programs in Virginia used Antabuse, a medicine that made people sick when combined with alcohol. There were some private recovery programs that followed the 12-step paradigm. However paperwork, lack of licensed staffing and the absence of quality services made it difficult for these private programs to stay open.

One of our resident priests was an outstanding homilist and retreat leader who was in demand all over the nation. He traveled alone constantly with no oversight, which ultimately led to heavy drinking. I can't count the number of times he woke me from a sound sleep to carry on about his football days in college. He also hallucinated that rats were running across his body and snakes were trying choking him. He would flail at these imagined attackers, and I would get calls from many a bartender who understandably saw his antics as a threat to other patrons. Then he would turn his anger on me. This man was extremely talented, but still susceptible to the progressive, insidious disease of addiction. And he was not alone.

Every day, addicted clients in our gym shelter experienced withdrawal symptoms leading to physical confrontations with others. The next day, they would tell me how much they appreciated my help. One left me with 17 stitches. The next morning, he had coffee with me and told me how much he appreciated my help. After experiencing firsthand the drastic behavioral swings induced by drugs and alcohol, I started searching for answers. Why did people let this happen to themselves?

How Do You Solve a Problem Like Maria?

As I mentioned earlier, our housekeeper Maria Lupian was the person in charge at the rectory. Maria was a Polish woman who had spent nine torturous years in a Nazi concentration camp in her home country. She was assigned to a crew building railroads. Day after day, she wielded an 18-pound sledgehammer, driving in railroad spikes into the ground.

This ordeal left her with muscular biceps and a damaged personality. She trusted very few people, other than priests. We learned of her family, the violence they had experienced, and about relatives who had been killed in the concentration camp. After being freed, Maria was sent to the Albany Diocese for relocation and a paid job through Catholic Charities. This was part of a national response to find safe housing and employment for homeless causalities of the war. Under a contract guaranteed by the diocese, Maria would remain with us at the parish for the remainder of her life.

There was a language barrier, but fortunately we had Olga Kulchofky and John Tatko to translate concerns and instructions to Maria. Olga and John handled food service in the rectory, which we used as a halfway house, with outside clients and priests residing together. We housed 24 people on the top two floors. It was also a social center, with offices in the basement and social services and a kitchen on the first floor.

Luckily, Father McKeon and I were on Maria's trusted list. She was respected and feared by all who met her. Nothing fazed her, not even the huge grain-silo rats that invaded our rectory when the city demolished some storage towers across the street. Maria would simply sweep the rats into the front vestibule, pound on them with her fist and remove the remains as if it were nothing.

Living at St. John's with Maria was one of the most challenging parts of my ministry. She had arrived in 1945 and never left the rectory in the 18 years I lived there. I quickly learned that she was the boss. She would walk around all day with a baseball bat, and whenever anyone tried to steal food from the kitchen or failed to heed her suggestions, she did not hesitate to use it.

Our rectory was always open to visitors who needed a meal. Sometimes hungry walk-ins attempted to take more than their fair share. Some tried to steal large cans of food or other items that could be traded for a bottle of wine on the street. While Maria was always eager to feed people, stealing was something she did not tolerate. That's why she always carried the bat.

At five feet, six inches tall and 258 pounds, Maria bore scars from the beatings she had received in the Nazi concentration camp. A number tattooed on her muscular arm served as a grim reminder. Imprisonment had prevented her from developing the skills of a traditional domestic employee. Her cooking was limited to Polish dishes or a simple chicken dinner. She always wanted to please the elderly Father McKeon, whose health was declining. She kept trying to make him eat more than he wanted. It was a nightly debate, with her yelling at our pastor in Polish to clean his plate.

Maria's meals left a lot to be desired. Sensing this, our neighbors frequently stopped by with goodies to keep us well fed. Bill Lombardo, owner of the legendary Albany Italian restaurant Lombardo's, would fill up two buckets of pasta with sauce for our needy residents in the rectory. Then-Father Howard Hubbard and I would make nightly trips to Lombardo's to pick up the free food. We had hundreds more homeless people in our many parish buildings and feeding them was always a challenge.

Some of our experiences with Maria were scary. More often than we care to remember, priests and visitors would need to rush to the hospital to have their stomachs pumped out after consuming one of her meals. When riots in the South End destroyed the grocery store that delivered food to the rectory, Maria had to be taken to the supermarket to shop. Polish-speaking parishioner John Tatko would escort her and let her wander the aisles alone with a shopping cart—but she didn't know how to read. Consequently, she came home with many "interesting" ingredients. Once she basted a chicken with Lestoil, mistaking it for cooking oil. Our kitchen exploded and firefighters had to come put out the fire. For the same meal, she put liniment on our salads and furniture polish in our coffee cream container. According to our recollections, Maria never attempted to learn any English. So we got by using sign language or asking for things in our very limited Polish.

When Maria was mad, she would hide the food, as she did when we had guests one Thanksgiving and she became angry with another Polish person who told her she was stupid. When my mom would visit and ask for a cup of tea, Maria would fetch the hot water, then reach into her bra and pull out a tea bag. On another occasion, mom went into Maria's kitchen to show her how to cut and prep meat. Maria proceeded to accidentally slice off mom's finger! Mom rushed out of the kitchen holding her finger in her hand and screamed, "Get me to the hospital immediately."

Sometimes Maria's frugal nature produced amusing results. She was always fond of celebrating birthdays. One year, on October 31, we made big sheet cake for Father Hubbard's birthday. Eight months later, we celebrated the final days of the legislative session by inviting several state legislators to dinner. I asked Maria to serve some cake for dessert, since we always had leftover baked goods donated by local bakeshops. Maria left the room and returned shortly with Father Hubbard's eight-month-old birthday cake! Since it had not been completely finished, she had stowed it under her bed. When I spotted Father Hubbard's name on the cake, it was quickly removed it and I went out to get ice cream for our guests.

On another morning, I invited several state legislators to breakfast at the rectory to submit a bill for their consideration. Senator Walter Langley had already arrived by the time I returned from Mass. I decided to run out and get some baked goods for the group, leaving the senator to greet the others. While I was gone, Maria came downstairs, saw my guests gathering in "her" kitchen and defaulted to her baseball-bat routine. It was a cold January day and, as I arrived home from the bakery, I saw Maria on the front steps waving her bat at the legislators, who were standing outside shivering.

In the late 1950s, prostitutes would roll their window shades up or down to indicate whether they were available for hire or busy with a customer. Maria liked to pass time sitting in her bedroom window at the rectory. Prospective "Johns" driving around the neighborhood would see her and she would say hello and "dobja," which meant "good" in Polish. Some interpreted this as an invitation and would come into the rectory. Maria would bring them to my office where a priest in clerical garb was the last thing they expected to see. I would tell them they needed to go elsewhere—this was a Catholic rectory, not a brothel.

"Lucky"

At St. John's, with its numerous parish buildings, we averaged about 18 break-ins a month. These incidents meant getting flashlights and investigating who might be involved. Frequently, it would a homeless person looking for a place to warm up. Sometimes they came to steal and a confrontation would ensue. I decided I needed a police dog. In the *Times Union* newspaper, I read about a woman who was moving and needed a good home for her dog. I called her and she was initially delighted by the idea of her dog living in a rectory. Until I told her that the church was on Green Street. She said she wouldn't allow her dog to live in our neighborhood. We kept looking and eventually found a stray named "Lucky." He was a winner, trained by Pop Johnson, manager of our AA clubhouse. Lucky would greet people at the front door and bark if he smelled alcohol.

The Political Machine and Governing Albany

Dan O'Connell was head of the Democratic Party in Albany County and ruled over every piece of turf in the city. He knew what was going on at all times. When infamous bootlegger Jack "Legs" Diamond decided to set up shop in Albany because it was strategically located between Canada and New York City, things did not end well for him. According to a Wikipedia entry: "Albany police killed Legs Diamond…because he didn't take Dan's advice and leave town." Those days are well documented in author William Kennedy's book *O Albany.*

South End residents were willing watch agents for the police. They reported on any outsiders who came to Albany. While newspaper accounts about crime in our city were commonplace, we never worried about it in our parish community. The people who operated in "unsanctioned" illegal activities were always outsiders who would be reported to the cops and dispatched with.

A private car came around to collect fees paid by some of our local businesses to ensure the safety of their brothels and gaming halls. They even united to make it impossible for any competition from outsiders to gain a foothold. They would defend the madams and stop any new streetwalkers coming in from out of town.

Albany's political powers were always proud that they were able to keep organized crime out while protecting locals involved in approved illegal activities. The locals were also expected to give police any information about dangerous outsiders. I knew that if I needed to speak with a local cop, I would find him in one of the bars getting updates from an informant. Outsiders were always shut down quickly and banished from town. Gangs were never permitted. Everyone was happy.

Dan O'Connell's political influence was far-reaching. Just after my arrival at St. John's, I stopped by a large community meeting at the school, just to see what was happening. There was nothing on their agenda having to do with the parish. Instead, I found them planning ways to control voting in an upcoming election. The men were reviewing what each family in the neighborhood needed: work, medical assistance, a nursing home, a place to live. They knew single person within the boundaries of their voting districts.

At the time, the City of Albany was completing five new 12-story public housing apartment buildings a block from our church. I suggested using some yellow brick in them, and I'm happy to see it as I drive past the buildings. These men reviewed all of the candidates for the new housing units to make sure that any potential occupants were registered with the Democratic Party.

Local politicians knew who lived in the community and they expected loyalty from them on Election Day. They would often respond to parishioners' needs by sending a note to the Albany Department of Social Services authorizing some sort of action on their behalf. It was a gesture of charity and a tool for accountability. Political power rested in the hands of local representatives. They decided who would get a tax increase and who would receive favors: a job, food baskets or home heating oil, among other things. Ward leaders visited every home and reported on what was being done to help those particular residents.

These local leaders used their influence with city and county leaders to ensure they achieved their desired results. It was actually a very responsive system that gave residents a measure of respect. Any calls I made to the mayor or commissioners on behalf of our neighbors usually resulted in immediate action to address the problem. Thanks to this system, our community responded with close to 90 percent support for the Democrats.

Outright welfare was a rare thing in Albany at the time, and Dan O'Connell's plan for job creation was, well, creative. It was often said that Albany City Hall had more janitors than the Empire State Building in New York City. People could receive favors, but they needed to work for them. There were no handouts; Dan always believed in the dignity of a paycheck.

Our political leaders knew the folks asking for help. They knew whether they were drinking their days away, or just having a run of bad luck. They would visit anyone seeking a helping hand to see what could be done. While many negative articles have been written about Dan O'Connell questioning his style, the people who lived in the South End of Albany respected his name and deeds.

As an advocate for South End residents, I was often considered a troublemaker and told to stay off of Dan O'Connell's turf. My barber, Charles Mufale, had a shop close to our church. He would let me know whether Dan was pleased or disappointed with me at any given time. Luckily, my mother's good friend Mary Marcy was an enthusiastic defender of my advocacy for the disenfranchised and a close friend of Dan's. She would smooth things over if I said anything against his administrative style. I never met or spoke with Dan in person because he was someone who could control me, and I wanted to avoid dependence on him for anything.

I recall an incident that caused Father McKeon to reconsider his support for the city administration. While in the hospital, Father McKeon requested an absentee ballot so he could vote. The ballot he received was already filled out with all of the Democratic candidates' names checked. He was simply asked to sign it. When he brought the filled-out ballot to the attention of the elections commissioner he was told, "I don't see the problem." From that day forward, Father McKeon refused to support the city administration.

After Dan O'Connell's death, most felt that the power structure fueled by favors and payoffs was beginning to crumble. Governor Thomas Dewey's administration, with its focus on oversight, exposed the illegal practices that had become business as usual. They gave way to competitive appointments, civil service rules and the elimination of the rewards system used to curry favor with voters. With this came less care for the poor and needy. Many people who had received jobs and other goodies in the past began to suffer.

PART II
Immersion into Ministry

A Multifaceted Ministry Begins

The Sisters of Charity created a solid academic program for students who attended our parish school. During my tenure, non-Catholic children accounted for 93 percent of the school's enrollment, and our loyal parishioners raised money to help fund their education.

There were, in reality, two separate ministries: a typical Catholic parish and a social services center. This combination helped break down most perceived racial differences.

My priestly duties expanded rapidly, and I ended up hiring several outstanding Black staff, starting with new teachers for our parish school. Loretta Parsons was humorous with a wonderful personality. Odell Thompson worked at the school and for the parish outreach youth programs. We hired several of Odell's 14 brothers and his one sister. (We called her the "family princess.") We developed a great staff of more than 50 people who, along with the Sisters of Charity, all worked together to assist the thousands of people who came knocking on our door. Many of the young people I meet now say "thank you for the help" that the Church extended to their grandparents.

We were always busy finding housing and support services for people migrating from the south. They arrived homeless and our staff helped them secure housing and employment. This became a large part of our ministry at St. John's. We were considered an outreach community center serving the poor and needy. Governor Rockefeller appointed me to many federal committees, which enabled me to develop important connections in state government. Those relationships helped me improve poor neighborhoods through the establishment of many new agencies.

Among Neighborhood Bars and Clubs

Owners and bartenders in our Green Street neighborhood never wanted to call the cops. At the time, the least expensive all-night private club was Spanish Joe's, which received a lot of press. Located at Herkimer and Franklin streets, around the corner from the Blue Note Bar, Joe's offered a combination of prostitution, gaming and drugs. The patrons were all bargain shoppers and the owner, Jesus Quaquacaro, catered to their addictions by keeping prices low. There was always a large container of stew on the bar so nobody would get hungry and leave.

Led by Olivia Rorie, families living close to Spanish Joe's pledged to fight for a safer neighborhood. They would eventually form the Herkimer Neighborhood Association and recruit help from outside of the area: college students and supporters like Dottie Anne Kite and Father Bonaventure, a Siena priest. Eventually they convinced the police to close Spanish Joe's. Despite this small victory, another club named Rabbits continued to provide the same type of low-cost services and took many of Joe's customers.

In the 1950s, the upper Green Street area was home to a long line of legitimate businesses. These establishments had teamed up to keep criminal elements out. Local college and law school students often gathered in the bars of upper Green, near Madison Avenue. I would walk in to fetch some of my "friends" who had wandered off to bring them home, and the students would help me load them into my 15-passenger van. Appropriately, the van had "Sobering up Center" painted on its side.

One very cold night, we picked up a guy because we were concerned for his safety. Turns out the man was a state legislator and he decided to sue me. Because of the lawsuit, the diocese ordered me to do this kind of work under my own name to avoid the fiscal exposure for the church.

Bob's Grill, another popular bar, sat on the corner of Division and Green streets. One night, a daily visitor at our free lunch program named Mary got cut up at Bob's. One of her friends called me and I and quickly went down to find a bloody scene. It was known that Mary hid her money in her sock, and some guy who needed cash for drugs had cut off her shoe and severely injured her in the attack. When I saw Mary lying on the floor bleeding, I lost it. I began grabbing guys who I suspected might have cut her.

Slim, a six-foot-six bartender, calmed me down and helped me put Mary in my car so I could take her to the hospital. After Mary was all stitched up, I had time to think about my rage against the men in the bar. The confrontation was actually a result of my failure to understand their disease. Drunks do stupid things to get another drink or drug. Later, I went back to Bob's Grill and told them all that I should not have lost my temper and they were quick to understand.

When Mary was released from the hospital, she immediately returned to Spanish Joe's on crutches to rest up. She just couldn't stay away. Soon after, she and a friend were found dead and covered with maggots behind one of our buildings. The troubling sight of poor Mary's lifeless body was a horrifying reminder of her addiction. All of Bob's drinking clientele attended her funeral, as did a reporter who had written about her tumultuous life on Green Street. The guy who had cut her apologized as she lay in the casket. After the service, we gathered in our parish yard for food and fellowship—no alcohol.

Recovery Aftercare Programs

The Pier Hotel, on Hudson Avenue at Green Street, was our best housing option for recovery aftercare programs. It offered safer parking than lower Green and could accommodate large Alcoholics Anonymous meetings. We housed 38 of our more stable residents there in private rooms. The hotel was surrounded and supported by members of 12-step programs and offered three open meetings a day.

With the help of those 12-steppers, we established many other agencies to support people with addictions: Project Lift, which offered residential opportunities; New Horizons; the Albany Council on Alcoholism (which became the Addiction Care Center of Albany); Hospitality House; Equinox; St. Peter's Addiction Rehabilitation Center (SPARC); Big Brothers and Big Sisters of New York State; and several other nonprofit community agencies. The most important programs created by us and funded by the state included 19 addiction treatment centers and crisis care services for the addicted. The state administered these programs freeing up our staff to concentrate on delivering services instead of managing finances.

People still actively drinking or using drugs were housed on the gym floor with the hope they would improve and decide to accept help. When that happened, they were moved upstairs to a room in our school building or at the rectory. If they demonstrated a commitment to stop using, they would be rewarded with a private room at the Pier Hotel. The different levels of lodging were used to reward those who showed progress toward recovery.

All of this was made possible by our second church collection and by my family's unexpected but welcome investment income. Gains from stocks and other assets enabled us to expand services independently for over 20 years. My investment portfolio increased by 90 percent over that span.

I preferred to keep this quiet, but eventually it became known that I had donated millions of dollars to fund addiction-recovery programs over the years. It was deeply satisfying to see how many lives were saved and restored by the programs and agencies I founded and funded. Many remain successful today, offering outstanding programs at numerous sites.

A New Way of Thinking

We desperately needed a voice in New York State to alter the way people thought about public intoxication, and to demonstrate that alcoholism was a disease—not a crime or a sin.

R. Brinkley Smithers, a recovering alcoholic who used his personal and family fortune to create the nation's largest foundation in support of alcoholism research and treatment, encouraged U.S. Senator Harold Hughes to work with me. We found forums where we could speak about alcoholism as an illness and health problem. Senator Hughes eventually sponsored a Uniform Act in Congress that promoted a medical model for alcoholism and did change many health laws.

My focus was the removal of "sinful thinking" from the discussion about why people became alcoholics, a popular opinion shared by most church communities and temperance organizations. My detractors ridiculed me and cast me as radical just looking for attention, not a priest. Radio host Bill Edwardsen of WGY invited me to respond most Sunday nights on his talk show. It was a full evening of debate with callers and it worked. We fielded genuine requests for help and people in recovery welcomed the opportunity to share their stories with others seeking assistance.

We expanded the aftercare program when I purchased 12 acres of property at 90 McCarty Avenue, formerly the site of the Hospital for Incurables. We moved the housing program from the Pier Hotel to this location, where I founded a new addiction care center and served as board chair for 29 years. George Schindler, our Vesta board attorney, later resigned his regular job to work on our new program that included housing, vocational training and treatment, otherwise known as Peter Young Housing, Industries and Treatment (PYHIT). More on George later.

Beginning in 1959, I spent much of my free time and energy at the State Capitol advocating for the decriminalization of public intoxication and the recognition of alcoholism as a disease. My ultimate goal: legislation that prescribed treatment for addiction, not incarceration.

The Challenges of the 1960s and Priestly Support

As a priest working in the South End of Albany for more than half a century, I was always concerned about how to show respect for people seeking assistance. In the 1960s, volunteers at St. John's parish counseled people in need and coordinated their applications. The St. Vincent De Paul Society and the Ladies of Charity of St. John's would split up the requests for assistance and go out to visit the applicants. They saw it as a Gospel opportunity.

As the demand for assistance grew, the bishop tasked Father

Howard Hubbard with opening a community outreach center on South Pearl Street. It was a great personal benefit to me to have Father Hubbard move into the rectory and witness firsthand the plight of the needy, angry people I worked with every day. And the outreach center he opened turned out to be a major advantage for our community. He would do anything to support our clients and parish. When he realized the magnitude the drug problem in our area, he put all of his energy into a special new drug recovery program called Hope House.

Fr. Hubbard also steadied me at a time when I was overcome by anger about not being able to assist all of the people in trouble. If we are humble and appreciate all of our gifts and blessings, we can grow in love for and gratitude to God, even as we mourn the suffering of others.

I had my share of difficulties with public authorities and employers who failed to respect and support our disadvantaged community. I would launch overly impassioned attacks in demanding that these people be respected and afforded the opportunity to pursue the American dream. I joined civil rights demonstrations, offending many people who would send anonymous letters claiming that I was not a Catholic priest, but instead a disgrace to the church.

It was invaluable to have Fr. Hubbard as a sounding board and confidant. We would escape to a nearby Howard Johnsons Restaurant after finishing our appointments to brainstorm ways the church could further assist the community. Fr. Nellis Tremblay, who was working nearby in the Arbor Hill area, would usually join us. These two priests, along with a great volunteer named Bill Murray, helped me vent, calm down and understand what the ministry of a priest needed to prioritize.

Early in my ministry, I discovered that any frivolous activities by newly ordained priests were discouraged. One evening I was taking a walk with another cleric when the bishop drove past. Back then, all priests were required to be in clerical dress in public at all times, and that included a black fedora. The bishop happened to catch me without my black hat. The diocesan chancellor called me the next day to remind me about the expectation of proper dress whenever in public.

Still young and uncomfortable with authority, I feared that if I played baseball or softball, I would be reported to the chancery for another round of fraternal correction. Yet, I was quickly learning that my ministry would not rise or fall because of a dress code, or be taken down by participation in secular activities. Stepping out of character now and then actually seemed to enhance my credibility as a person who was approachable and available to help.

Growing up, I dreamed about playing professional baseball. In my early days as a priest, I remained passionate about playing ball with longtime friends in the Albany Twilight League. Sports had always been a blessing in my life. Now, it enabled me to make new friends and develop contacts that would be valuable to me both as a person and as a priest. But senior clergy thought that a priest playing semi-pro ball or shooting hoops at 11 o'clock in the evening was not only a waste of time, it was detrimental to the demeanor expected of one who was engaged in advancing the mission of the church.

I was personally conflicted. Almost from the beginning, out of a sense of moral justice, I wanted to be involved in community activities of all kinds. While some felt the image of the priesthood should be protected without compromise, I was inclined to see my ministry as a bridge to the community.

My parish and teaching duties prevented me from traveling to many civil rights demonstrations, not to mention protests opposing the Vietnam War. This turned out to be a lucky consequence for me, because many priests who led movements and demonstrations found themselves in trouble with church leaders or government authorities. I learned a valuable lesson during these years: stay focused on your primary target.

Closing the Brothels

Although most of my ministry was dedicated to helping people cope with alcohol or heroin addiction, for many years I tried to improve the lives of the women and men employed by Albany's madams and gambling halls.

Most brothels kept a bouncer around, usually a large man who resided in the basement under filthy conditions. The bouncer was always on call to prevent customers from abusing the women. The prostitutes had a bell they could ring to summon help if a customer became unruly or threatening. Whenever that bell rang, the bouncer would streak upstairs wielding a club to calm things down and avoid involving the police. The madams paid the bouncers with a free room, free wine and free food.

I complained about the brothels often to the district attorney, the city administration and county officials. Their point of view about them went something like this: "This type of activity in the city is inevitable, but we're trying to limit it to only those few blocks in the South End." They wanted me, as a pastor, to earn the trust of the bouncers in hopes they would keep me and the police informed. Such inside information might be useful in heading off trouble and helping people in distress.

My routine around this time was to be in Police Court right when the judge asked for the morning lineup of people charged with public intoxication (usually 50 to 60 defendants). "Do you want to go to jail or to Father Young's program?" the judge would ask, somewhat rhetorically. We would then lead a parade of accused offenders from the court to our shelter program at St. John's. This was a great opportunity for us to steer these people toward recovery.

We would hold regular morning meetings where people in our program could share stories about their experiences in the gambling halls, brothels and drug dens. Our staff would immediately get them into one of our recovery programs. Ironically, they would often come to me to resolve their turf differences nonviolently since we could handle the cost of their bail through bondsmen Bill Bernardo and Herbie Goldstein, one of my classmates from Siena.

Every night local streetwalkers greeted the never-ending parade of cars filled with men seeking their services. The women stood in front of their brothels with flashlights and their coats open, displaying their bodies to potential customers, and slowing down the flow of traffic to discuss the price of their services.

After six years at St. John's, all of our attempts to close the brothels had failed. Then, one evening after our eighth-grade school programs had let out, a predator picked up one of our female students. She was later found behind Hackett Public School, raped and murdered. This time I was not about to take "no" for an answer. We finally rallied enough community support to shut down the brothels in our neighborhood for good.

Making Progress

There was much to criticize about how the old Albany political machine operated under Dan O'Connell. That said, I often wonder if the current bureaucracy's tactics for assisting the poor and needy are an improvement, or simply replacing one flawed system with another.

Under the old system, politicians knew their neighborhoods and the residents who voted. They would show up with a 3 x 5 card to remind people who to vote for on Election Day. In turn, their needs would receive prompt attention.

Today, it seems people in need are just numbers in a long line. Many forms must be filled out in order to obtain assistance from state or local governments, and anger can erupt out of frustration. There are not enough funds to go around and the competition for resources is fierce. Amid all of this, perhaps we have lost our sense of community in taking care of those less fortunate.

The availability of funding for our programs improved during the era of President Lyndon B. Johnson. And those federal dollars were matched by state and county funds, which made it possible for us to expand. We had more than 100 people a day showing up for help. All we required was a first name and a description of their need, then a staff volunteer would see to them personally.

Later, Social Services began asking county agencies for a complete accounting of each client's information as a condition for funding. Our intake dropped by 95 percent because people were afraid to share their private information due to outstanding arrest warrants for other "complications." Due at least in part to this reluctance, crime in the area escalated as people became desperate for money to meet emergency and even their basic needs.

These programs certainly had their shortcomings. On Thanksgiving Day, for example, our St. Vincent DePaul Society men would sometimes notice five or more baskets of food from neighboring agencies delivered to the same individual or family. To stop this abuse of the system, all of the agencies began sharing listings to prevent people from taking advantage of the giving season.

We were able to increase our food bank donations through the generous cooperation of Lewis Golub, whose family operated Price Chopper Supermarkets. Lew was a classmate of mine at Siena College. Here again, experienced hustlers knew they could trade donated food items for a bottle of cheap wine. Now, even food stamps can be traded for cigarettes and alcohol at some stores.

With the constant need to expand services to the homeless, our volunteers opened up more than 15 new small shelter buildings in 1964. One day, I bought 50 new chairs for our shelter at the old Pier Hotel. When I came back that night, there were only three left. Ralph, our manager, got drunk and sold the rest for $50. The power of addiction strikes again!

Changes in the Church

Many changes in the church came about during the Second Vatican Council. Priests faced the congregation for Mass and the liturgy was prayed in the languages of the people. We spoke to the congregation in English. The Vatican II changes also allowed Catholics to pray with other denominations, encouraged friendships with non-Christian faiths and reinforced a sense of mission in the church.

Many of my unorthodox activities had caught the attention of the chancery over the years. I was called in more than once, reprimanded and reminded about what a priest ought to be. The model of priesthood in that day meant you stayed above the fray of everyday struggles. But now, the Second Vatican Council called for more of a grassroots church. This was right in my wheelhouse. Because of my involvement in social ministry, I was elected president of the newly formed Priests Council of New York State (PCNY). This was something new for all priests, as the presbyteries became more vocal.

I set out to coordinate a statewide effort to build a social ministry tract, so we could all learn from each other and bond in our Catholic efforts to serve the needy. Many different voices were already showing support for various movements. My friend Father Daniel Berrigan, SJ, ascended to a leadership role in protesting the Vietnam War while teaching at LeMoyne College in Syracuse, New York. I was with him and his brother Phil, also a priest, for numerous panel discussions on social justice issues. However, my concerns centered more on racial injustice, job barriers and the economic concerns that undermined those on the fringes of society.

I was re-elected president of PCNY and became the spokesperson for thousands of priests in the state. To say I was seen as a threat is an understatement. I was a lightning rod! In a meeting of the Baltimore National Federation of Priests Council, there was a debate about optional celibacy for priests. The discussion made the national news, and when I arrived home, there was a note for me to go see Bishop Edward Maginn, no matter the hour of my arrival.

The bishop had seen the news item, which referenced me saying that celibacy should be optional. Bishop Maginn was displeased that the priests council, seen by our diocese as a consultative body, was making public statements about liberal viewpoints without first checking with local church authorities. He lectured me all night long until I asked to be excused. I had to celebrate morning Mass and then report for another full day of teaching at Cardinal McCloskey High School. He was very upset.

The next day I attended the annual dinner of First Friday Club, for which I served as chaplain. The event always attracted the most powerful Catholic and community leaders in the City of Albany. I was at the head table when the bishop arrived. When he saw me, he told the president of the club to have me removed. I left quickly. The next morning, I was once again summoned to see Bishop Maginn. I was expecting another disciplinary lecture, but instead he apologized for banishing me from the dinner and admitted that he had acted hastily. He also asked me to join him out for dinner more often to demonstrate our unity in the priesthood. He became one of my closest and most admired friends.

The World in Black and White

The early 1960s were difficult years. Our challenges were unique as we experienced the changing—and charged—world of "Black and white" relationships. Before closing our parish grammar school, enrollment had gone from 90 percent white students to 96 percent Black within a two-year period. As our parish was predominately white, I admired their willingness to donate time and money to support a mostly Black inner-city school.

Our white community comprised mostly Italians. They knew how to put on events that provided the resources needed to keep a quality education program up and running. The Sisters of Charity also assisted. They were just the right folks to be helping the poor. It was their mission. They created an experimental "William Glasser Education Model" of small classes and innovative special-education ideas.

We took in dropouts from local public schools and demonstrated that we could prepare them to succeed. To this day, I meet people who came through St. John's and are doing very well. They remember and remark about how they benefited from the sisters and the dedicated lay staff.

There were so many areas of need in the community—I didn't know which way to turn first. I tried to prioritize my efforts to aid the addicted after meeting with street people and local clergy. But it was very frustrating. I was feeling isolated from the white community and the political establishment as I became more involved in my social ministry. I felt like many of those who took up the struggle for civil rights. I was committed to the leadership of Dr. Martin Luther King, Jr. and had the privilege of being on the National Mall in Washington, D.C., on August 28, 1963, as Dr. King delivered his prophetic "I Have a Dream" speech.

The organizer of that march on Washington was A. Philip Randolph. Twenty years later, I was appointed co-chair with him of a federal program created by the Comprehensive Employment Training Act of 1973, or CETA. I worked with this historic labor leader for 16 years. He focused his efforts in New York City, while I attempted to promote employment opportunities upstate through the State Department of Labor's implementation of CETA.

I also admired Whitney Young, a civil rights leader from the Urban League, only nine years my senior. Dr. King and Whitney Young were bridge-builders between our divided white and Black society of the 1960s. While they worked to develop employment programs for their constituents, more militant advocates of Black power were caught up in street riots and violence. I chose to avoid involvement with this type of leadership.

Being a white priest in a Black community was challenging. One experience in particular helped me better understand the anger of many inner-city residents. Through the Priests Council of New York, I was offered an invitation to attend a conference in New Orleans. It was held at a retreat house just outside the city. Upon arrival, we were told to change into ragged old clothing that the presenters provided—and that was just the beginning. We had to sleep on the floor. When we ate, we were given no dishes or utensils. We ate with our fingers as we sat on the ground.

Meanwhile, the Black participants were dressed in freshly laundered clothes, assigned seats at the conferences and took their meals at tables with white linens and china. It provided us with sobering insights about how slaves had been treated and helped us feel what it was like to be excluded from simple, basic privileges. We were abused and screamed at for the duration of the conference, and many of us left. The experience helped me connect with the feelings of so many people would try to help along the way as a bridge-builder.

Whenever I could find the time, I would make it a point to play night basketball in our gym or on the courts in the housing projects. I was trying to lose some weight, but playing ball also gave me an opportunity to meet most of the young men in the area, who were predominately Black. They soon felt comfortable with me and our conversations would often turn to their worries about getting a job or how they needed extra help in school. I tried to help the better athletes secure scholarships and get them involved with Albany's many Pop Warner football and Babe Ruth baseball leagues sponsored by our parish.

As time went on, I could see the increasing need to engage with our youth to keep them out of trouble. Our parish became a major recreation center in the city. It motivated me to create a number of youth programs, some with federal funding, in coordination with city youth bureaus: camps and summer activities, arts and crafts, tutoring and school programs, the St. Vincent de Paul Society's nightly visits to the needy, the Big Brothers and Big Sisters Program. We had carpenters, painters and dozens of others—53 paid employees in all—who wanted to assist. Many energized youths also wanted to contribute. Organizing them was a job in itself! They were eager to become part of the solution and not part of the problem, and their underlying anger manifested as amazing energy.

Life became more complicated and challenging as these tumultuous years unfolded. The redlining of property in the South End by banks discouraged white people from living there, compelling them to leave for safer parts of the city or the suburbs. At the same time, living conditions in the Deep South were difficult, so Black people were heading north hoping to find more job opportunities than in the segregated south. An ever-growing number of transplants were arriving at the bus station in Albany from South Carolina and Mississippi, as well as the Caribbean.

The neighboring church of my dedicated friend Elder Jack Johnson and our Church of St. John became a first friendly stop for those who had just arrived in Albany. Our staff would house them and send them to our social services team to help them get a start with food, clothing and a job. Elder Jack Johnson demonstrated a love of all people and always tried to help.

For 17 years, I was vice president of the Interdenominational Ministers Association or, as the city called it, "the Black Ministers Association." We often held brainstorming sessions on how to assist residents of the South End. Frequently these meetings would become contentious, especially among younger folks of different colors. More often than I care to remember, I would find myself caught up in their physical confrontations. At 287 pounds and in great shape, I was usually able to defuse the disagreements.

I continued to work toward removing the barriers that prevented people from having access to equal opportunities for employment, housing and other essential services. My goal has always been to empower the disenfranchised to succeed and become productive members of American society. It was my ministry to implement the Beatitudes. One could call it fighting for the underdog, but to me it was the Gospel and the work that we are all called to do.

Bill Murray, a retired director at the State Civil Service Department, volunteered at St. John's every day, along with several other recently retired state-commissioner-level friends. They took a hands-on role responding to the needs of the 150-plus needy folks who appeared at our parish door daily, asking for help and, most often, seeking employment.

Bill and his friends told me that I was internalizing the pain of those I served, and it was making me an angry guy. They weren't wrong. I would rail against authority about the countless number of people who needed a job, food, rent money, transportation and economic assistance. Where was social services?

Then there were those dealing with criminal justice issues, including people on parole or probation. Our volunteers would interview clients in order to assess their needs and find a way to respond. The more we found answers and assistance for those in desperate need, the more the word got out, and even more people would show up at our door.

I felt overwhelmed at times and angry that so few seemed to care. Fortunately, the volunteers calmed me down, and methodically we began to organize channels that would provide solutions. I set up even more new agencies and committees to tackle the problems of the poor—not the least of which was their health care. The lesson I learned was, "Don't try to go it alone." I needed to build a new constituency to make good things happen.

The Berlin Wall, the Vietnam War, the Watts riots and other national crises were all in the news. The City of Albany was caught up in the same societal anguish. I had to worry about race-based fights in the high schools. As chair of the Capital Area Human Relations Committee, I was presented with news of confrontations daily—

all symptoms of our divided society. Sometimes the confrontations resulted in physical beatings. There were often angry calls and letters expressing resentment about my involvement. Negative comments in the local media complained about my "lack of interest" in parish work, claiming I was just a social activist in priest's clothing. The label of "street priest" seemed to stick. While it didn't bother me, it was difficult to hear from mom and dad about what their friends were saying.

Being in the inner city gave me a very different view of ministry. At times, I responded in a very defensive manner. I felt alone in the South End, and I'm sure other priests working in Albany's inner-city parishes felt the same sense of isolation.

The other ministers and I held weekly meetings to help ease tensions between Black and white neighbors. At one of our better-publicized meetings, we welcomed the leaders of the State University of New York's Black Studies Program. Sadly, the head of the program refused to shake my white hand as he stood before the crowd dressed in a dashiki and holding a walking stick. But all of the ministers quickly rallied around our togetherness as Christians and urged their most vocal leader to accept me.

In fact, most of the separatism ideas came from the university. As was stated: "They did not live here and were not around to stop the anger they created" in our neighborhoods.

Albany Mayor Erastus Corning 2nd employed a few Black leaders to keep the city administration informed and to quell any negative sentiments about his leadership. However, the Black ministers and I had to be strong in order to effect some necessary changes.

Black militants once visited my South Ferry Street office insisting that I leave the neighborhood, along with all other white people, so they could have an exclusively Black community. They were physically attacking me until Elder Jack Johnson and other Black ministers formed a blockade to protect me. All of the ministers in the South End came together as a group to calm racial differences. We were all busy clergy, but we took time to discuss how we could cooperate in addressing the racial needs of our communities. Although I was a white man, they accepted our parish and integrated us into their leadership circle. I had the advantage of being able to rally needed support and raise money.

I always admired my mother and her openness about doing what she thought was right. At one point, I told her I was going on a bus trip to Boston and she joined me. Mom was expecting a visit to Filene's Basement for some shopping. I didn't tell her that our plans included joining a demonstration to march in support of school integration. As we marched, we were pelted with tomatoes and eggs. "What did you get me into?" asked mom. Well, I got her into many things, and she was just amazing. We always returned safe and unharmed.

At the time, I was chaplain to the local Elks Club and Knights of Columbus and a member of Wolfert's Roost Country Club. At a meeting of each club, I proposed that they begin admitting qualified Black people into their membership. I suggested some of the most prominent Black people in our Albany leadership, but all three organizations ignored my request. I kept pressing the point until they all became upset with me, and with my parents. Many of the leaders of these organizations were guys I had grown up with, but they couldn't fathom why I was making such an issue out of integration.

Some began to take out their frustration with me on my mother. They would yell at her to "get out of those radical groups" and stop pushing to allow Black people to be members. But the more they criticized mom, the more of an activist she became in the inner-city Black communities. She organized and coordinated many events in her home. I felt totally supported. Many a night, we would gather in mixed groups that mom had set up. Mom demonstrated such a positive approach. If a group resisted accepting certain people, she would have her own friends cross over boundaries to set the right example. She never rejected anyone, joined many integrated social clubs and became a sincere friend to so many.

Priests were pulled in many directions as we attempted to address problems in the community and provide leadership for the many concerns troubling our nation. On a typical day, I might be called upon to speak to the issue of migrant labor in the morning, citing the efforts of Cesar Chavez and the national union of farmworkers. Then, in the afternoon, I would be at an emergency meeting of our interdenominational ministers association, talking about fistfights in the schools between our Black and white students.

We priests felt isolated as the go-to people called upon to cool down hot debates. Local battles raging from 1964 through 1967 put me in the middle of people's differences every day. Meanwhile, I received no support from the city and mayor.

Some of our parishioners and some of my brother priests were confused and upset about the role I had taken on. They didn't see this work as part of our ministry. Parishioners did not expect their priest to march for integration. A conservative national Catholic newspaper called me nothing more than a social worker, accusing me of failing in my role as a priest.

I will admit that there were several events I participated in that I now regret. Some were local demonstrations that started out peacefully, but then people full of hatred, sometimes with guns, would disrupt the marchers. Some were members of the radical social change group Weathermen, who used violence to take advantage of our civic and community involvement. I frequently set up meetings with some of our elected leaders. I would arrive to find the room filled with strangers making angry demands. This happened with state commissioners, mayors and even Governor Nelson A. Rockefeller. Sometimes the State Police were called in to remove the protesters. Nonetheless, our meetings were always held for a cause and with just intentions.

Some of my close inner-city priest friends crossed a line with their activism and were sent to jail. Ironically, in 1983, the U.S. Conference of Catholic Bishops issued a "Peace Pastoral" that advocated for many of the issues that inner-city clergy had been fighting to advance for 20 years. Further, the U.S. bishops spoke out in a national letter titled "Economic Justice for All." We inner-city clergy felt like we were out ahead of the bishops' leadership. I'm delighted to say that our own bishops and state clerical leadership never told us to back off from our efforts to help the poor.

Keeping House (Systemic Change)

When Governor Rockefeller announced the construction of the Empire State Plaza, many of our neighbors had to give up their homes to make way for the new bridges and highways that would provide access to the plaza. Construction of the plaza and the I-787 highway made new housing in the South End nearly impossible to find. Our neighborhood suffered severely from the devastating effects of mass demolition.

The state said it wanted to improve the streets in our neighborhood. They installed new streetlights and a tennis court, which I never saw anyone use. But none of the houses or other buildings received any significant repairs. I put a pool ball on the floor of the rectory and watched it roll quickly to the corner of the room, proving they hadn't corrected its structural problem. The buildings were left with the same old defects. The only big change was a new convoluted name for our neighborhood: "Steamboat Square" instead of the "Gut of Green Street."

During this period, I served on several New York State boards and commissions. I was appointed to a board for the protection of clients in public institutions by the governor's office. I also served on federal committees under Presidents John F. Kennedy and Lyndon B. Johnson.

Homeless people in the news were now a major concern, especially those who were drinking, wandering the streets begging for money and sleeping in doorways. Since promoting changes in our New York State mental health laws to replace incarceration with treatment, I was their voice. And I was more than happy to serve on a state board tasked with improving their care. As board members, we received intensive training on what to investigate and how to respond before touring the state.

I was assigned to work in upstate New York as an advocate for the homeless and developmentally disabled populations. Whenever a complaint was received by the state, I would visit the facility to investigate the concerns and if necessary bring them to the attention of the commissioners. My heroes were Dr. Christopher Terrence, Commissioner of the Office of Mental Health, and Dr. Ruth Fox, the first Director of the National Council on Alcoholism. They became two of my closest friends, and I truly respected their great work in the healthcare system with compassion for everyone.

My work on boards and commissions at the federal level opened up a whole new world for me. I would walk around the Capitol building with an old lobbyist friend and meet former state legislators who were now serving nationally. The experience introduced me to influential leaders who took an interest in their addicted and homeless constituents as well as those in the criminal justice system. Being in Washington, D.C. for the Voting Registration Act of 1965 was another highlight.

As I had mentioned, we left the Pier Hotel and moved to our new McCarty Avenue facility in order to house the hundreds of disenfranchised people in our area. There, we held Alcoholics Anonymous meetings and offered meals at no cost. I was able to operate the facility by encouraging guests in recovery to pitch in, and it was fun to feel that we were all making a difference.

Pat Howard, an old Irishman who stood only five-foot, four inches, was the director of the Pier Hotel. Pat received help maintaining order at the hotel from a huge, muscular guy named Arcel Kirk, who stood nearly a foot taller than his boss. Pat, with Arcel at his side, would tell clients that the house ran an alcohol- and drug-free program. If any problems arose, Arcel would be "handling" them.

Arcel was my close friend and stayed at our McCarty Avenue property in the old nurses' residence. Part of his charge was to protect the property. Tragically, an unidentified assailant who was visiting his family at the facility later murdered Arcel.

We eventually renovated buildings to expand our programs on this great 12-acre site. Sadly, the centerpiece of the campus—the abandoned Hospital of the Incurables—was torched one election night. Lacking the money to restore it, we had to tear it down, which dealt a major blow to our expansion plans. St. John's Parish, which provided all of the funds and staff, submitted a request to Albany County for a grant without success.

But that was far from the end for McCarty. In fact, the program grew from those early informal meetings into the first locally funded, nonprofit, certified alcoholism treatment center. I stayed on as founder and president for the next three decades. When I see it today, I am a very happy guy.

The Parish as an Oasis

Our parish took up a second collection every Sunday to pay for our outreach programs. I personally made up any shortfalls using my investment income, as alluded to earlier.

As time went on, other diocesan priests like Father Robert Roos were assigned to live in our rectory. That helped immensely, even when they had ministries apart from St. John's. I also enjoyed Saturday morning breakfast meetings with area Black ministers for 17 years. Bishop David Ball from the Episcopal Cathedral of All Saints, Rev. Bob Lamar from the Presbyterian Church and many other inner-city clergy of all denominations were united in a team effort to facilitate change. It's a shame that our conversations were never transcribed; we usually lamented about the confusion and chaos we dealt with each day!

At one point, *The Evangelist*, our diocesan newspaper, asked me to write an article about my concerns for inner-city ministry. It gave me a chance to let off some steam and ask for some empathy from the Catholic community. Many parish priests in more traditional assignments didn't understand inner-city ministry. They presumed we were just complaining about the problems, and everyone had problems. It was important to recognize that different approaches were required to serve diverse populations. If a ministry fails to account for ethnic differences, we lose those people. We cannot expect African Americans, Hispanics or others to easily settle into an Anglo-Saxon form of liturgy and ministry.

We learned this at St. John's in the 1960s. Every Sunday, we celebrated a traditional Mass, a gospel Mass and a Hispanic Mass. We attempted to unite the congregation through potluck meals and picnics. All three groups were people of faith, and we soon began to notice some of the "traditional" people dropping in for the gospel service or Spanish Mass—supposedly because "the music was different."

Our approach created an exciting, vibrant parish with people from different ethnic backgrounds actively participating. This was one of the goals set by the Vatican II Council, which sought to modernize the Catholic Church and make it more accessible. All of this was refreshing and fulfilling for me as a pastor. Black parishioners would work on the Italian dinners, and Italians would support the soul food festivals. It was a happy island of unity in a divided nation.

Parishioners with Problems

The 1960s were bizarre years. On the positive side, they produced many stories about people who overcame addiction—stories that inspired strength in others challenged by similar problems.

A former college friend, George Schindler, was one person who never forgot the help he received from St. John's. He was a very competent assistant attorney general for New York State, but he began to lose his battle with the bottle. I was sitting on the steps of one of our shelters on Clinton Avenue one hot summer evening when I saw this guy trying to make his way up the hill. He was having a more than difficult time maneuvering and ended up collapsing on the sidewalk near our house. I went over to help him. It was George looking up at me.

A couple of our residents, who themselves had been dry only

for a day or two, came over to help. George was in really bad shape, unshaven and nearly unclad. He had been sleeping in the park.

George started his road to recovery that night. He had a sincere desire to get sober and needed help. He went into detox and then to rehab at a Pennsylvania program called Chit Chat Farm run by Dick Caron, a recovering alcoholic who used his resources to help others. Dick provided his services for free.

Afterward, George came to live with us at St. John's rectory. He became a great asset, managing our finances and bookkeeping. He also rejoined the workforce, at first with a job mopping floors. Eventually he returned to his law career as a bill drafter and staff manager for the state legislature. George wrote most of the legislation related to recovery that was considered at the Capitol over a 30-year period. The bills he authored were outstanding because he took the time to perform due diligence and because they were informed by his own recovery experience.

After George retired, he volunteered to be president of our housing and property management arm, Vesta Community Housing Development Board Corporation. He demonstrated the type of authentic goodness that we often see emerge in people who have been homeless. Many who have passed through our halfway houses have dedicated their lives to helping others who are still sick and suffering.

George remained a close friend until the time of his death.

Cardinal McCloskey High School

In 1959, all young priests were appointed to teach in a diocesan Catholic high school. That in itself was arguably a full-time job, especially since the priests and sisters were expected to coordinate after-school activities, all on top of completing parish duties. But teaching for 10 years was my most relaxing ministry and the most joyful part of any day. I still love catching up with alumni and make it a point to attend reunions.

The Catholic school system, with its religious and lay staff, offered students an outstanding education at a low cost. My teaching tenure began just after the diocese consolidated several small parish high schools—St. John's, St. Anne's, St. Joseph's and Cathedral—into one central institution named Cardinal McCloskey High School. With responsibility for 1,200 to 1,300 students, our faculty included eight priests, many more sisters and only eight laypeople.

Since I had a background and interest in athletics, I was named the athletic director. I asked the principal, Father Bill Turner, what kind of budget we had for athletics. He told me I would have to raise funds on my own. Despite the unfavorable odds, we were able to field teams in all sports within one year. We also had more than 900 students participating in diocesan and intramural athletic programs. We raised the money to cover fees, bus transportation, uniforms and equipment by sponsoring dances and socials. We would hold two or more events a week to help meet expenses.

We were also very resourceful. For example, while soliciting donations for uniforms, I lucked out when a local college gave me all of its old football gear. The uniforms didn't quite fit our players, but the newly created Pep Club did some sewing and washing to solve the problem. The football team had to make do with just one coach, Clem Zotto. The same was true for all sports. Doctors donated their time to do team physicals, and parents in the PTA helped out with the socials and dances.

My philosophy was to keep the students busy and out of trouble. Almost all of them participated in after-school programs. We offered clubs and intramural activities, and in my 10 years of running those programs we never had a problem. It also gave us the joy of walking around and greeting the students, which helped us bond with them. For students who did not have the talent or appetite for athletes, the faculty ran a variety of clubs: camera, art, debate and drama, to name a few.

Rebellious behavior in those days might be girls rolling up their skirts to their knees to look more fashionable, and guys getting demerits for "pegging" their pants, chewing gum and sporting a duck-style haircut. When I ponder the problems of today, I often wonder, "What happened?"

During after-school activities, faculty members heard about students who might need help. Common signs were not having lunch money, drinking and hanging around with the wrong crowd. Often a little understanding and a friendly conversation would get them back on track. I made trips to New York City and Washington, D.C., to advocate for funding for school programs in addition to my work at the State Capitol and in the parish.

I was working so much at McCloskey and St. John's, and also very active helping the addicted and promoting desegregation, that I went to the chancery to see if I could be relieved of my teaching responsibilities. I was allowed to resign and devote all of my efforts to my parish ministry. While a necessary move, I've always missed the connection with the students and their activities.

When I went to the Capitol to change the law on public intoxication and to advocate for treatment, I found a great friend in Senator Ed Speno of Long Island. As chair of the finance committee, he supported addiction prevention and education at schools across the state. We traveled to all of the major cities in New York to hold hearings on our proposals, and the bills finally passed. BOCES programs received several million dollars to provide educational opportunities to all students, and a program was created to assist those who needed counseling.

Until his death in 1971, Senator Speno and I spent many years lobbying legislators to support bills that would help the addicted. Having taught the addiction education curriculum in high schools, I became a member of the State Association of Health Administrators and was twice honored with the New York State Educator of the Year award. But it was my partnership with Senator Speno that made it all possible.

Racial Tensions Flare

The times remained tense. Peer pressure on college students to be aggressive and bully was enormous. One day I loaned my car to some neighbors, and when they returned it, I noticed that the rear end was almost touching the pavement. So I opened the trunk and found it filled with guns. Seems my neighbors had in turn loaned the vehicle to some students from Springfield, Massachusetts, who used it to make a run for "supplies." This is how I was tipped off that a riot was about to happen.

I ran over to Mayor Erastus Corning's office to warn him of the imminent violence, but he wasn't there. I finally caught up with the mayor as he left the Fort Orange Club and told him about the angry students from local colleges and the agitators who were headed into town. He didn't seem worried or willing to speak with local Black leaders in an attempt to head off the unrest. So I started calling parents in the area.

The parents were much more responsive. They quickly assembled and started an all-night effort to organize, creating the "United Black Parents" group. They realized that if their kids obtained guns, the police would get machine guns; and if their kids got machine guns, the police would get cannons. They knew their kids would become casualties.

The outsiders moved in and took over the high schools: First Albany High, then Philip Schuyler in the South End. I was called in and found the school completely taken over. They set classrooms on fire and held me captive. When the neighborhood kids saw that I was in trouble, they came to my rescue. The bonds we had formed by working together every night in the gym paid off. We were able to calm things down and then a SWAT team came in and took control of the scene.

Buses were overturned and buildings destroyed. It was difficult to feel safe on the street. Special protective screens were installed on police cars to stop bricks from piercing their windows. Radicals from outside of the community had supplied our students with guns; many locals were jailed. Armed guards were placed at every corner in the downtown area. I thanked God for the wisdom of the United Black Parents. They were a dedicated group and had credibility in the community. It was them gaining control over their children that quelled the riots.

The United Black Parents wanted to call a meeting of all inner-city residents to air their differences with the city administration and school officials. I offered them the parish church as a possible site for the community meeting. When the mayor heard about my gesture, he and the chief of police paid me a visit. They told me me I couldn't host the meeting because they had issued an emergency order prohibiting public gatherings. I felt the meeting was essential in order to maintain the momentum of the United Black Parents group. I called Bishop Edward Maginn and told him of my intent to defy the order against the assembly. He said he trusted my decision.

We were all nervous. About 2,000 people filled the church and spilled outside where the media had gathered. The parents elected a team of Black leaders to represent the group under the direction of Vernell Allen, who was named chairperson. They took it upon themselves to fight peacefully for change and justice. In my estimation, this saved countless lives.

The meeting turned out to be the best thing that could have happened. These dedicated leaders continued to meet with the city administration, and many positive changes resulted from the discussions.

The discourse between community and city leaders wasn't always quite so civil and productive. I recall one incident that was particularly disturbing. There had been ongoing complaints about the high-rise housing in the neighborhood. They peaked when a young boy plunged 11 floors down an open elevator shaft to his death. Residents wanted to confront the mayor about this tragic accident, so I set up a meeting, but things turned ugly. They began swearing at the mayor, and ultimately a woman physically attacked him. At that point he had us escorted out with no resolution to the problem and television cameras recording it all.

Despite some unfortunate incidents, I'm proud of the role the church played during these difficult, revolutionary times. Bishop Maginn was a man of great integrity and we communicated daily. A group of very committed Black men known as the "Brothers" were often in the news, and I encouraged the bishop to understand their point of view. He tried to empathize, and even visited some of the activists in jail to hear their side of the story about events that led to their incarceration.

Later, Bishop Maginn made the unprecedented decision to pledge $100,000 from the annual Bishop's Appeal to fund programs to aid the Black community. Many Catholics at large resented this pledge, and contributions to the annual appeal suffered for years. I felt it was one of the best things that he had ever done.

Twinning

There were sincere people from more affluent parishes who wanted to help impoverished, inner-city communities. One concept gaining popularity in the church had real potential for raising their consciousness about the plight of those of the less fortunate: "twinning." An affluent parish would "twin" with an inner-city parish and become actively involved in caring for the poor.

In our case, when we combined committees from the twinned parishes to examine our efforts from social functions to liturgy, a very different set of priorities surfaced. I found myself defending the judgments of our inner-city members, while the suburban committee defended its structured style of planning and priorities. St. John's parishioners were used to responding to emergency needs with no time for a committee meeting to consider the issue.

Twinning also surfaced liturgical differences that showed up in the styles of our choirs. Our two parishes decided to combine choirs for a televised Mass to highlight our cooperation. But differences in their musical approaches resulted in major arguments moments before the cameras came on. Sadly, the director and some choir members from the suburban parish left because they did not want to be involved with our gospel music.

I remember thinking about how I could have resolved such differences of opinion and polarizing views. But the constant emergencies back home on Green Street took priority, and all of the committee meetings placed too many demands on our inner-city folks, who were working extra jobs just to support their families.

Bridging the different cultures of the two parish communities became even more problematic when we started discussing ways to help the needy people who came knocking on our door in the South End. Volunteers from the other parish would call at the last minute to say that something had come up and they couldn't cover their work assignment. But the people seeking help would always be there, and I needed volunteers I could depend on.

In Search of Aftercare Solutions

Addiction recovery is a long-term process that continues after treatment is over. Aftercare begins with providing guests in need with a stable, positive environment. Our St. John's Parish opened up hundreds of shelter beds in 1959, at first in our gym, and then later at other sites. Purchasing more buildings to increase capacity was always our mission.

We tried to find aftercare that would accept people from our homeless housing locations to expose them to peers who were street wise and willing to share their "experience, strength and hope." Programs operated by the Catholic Worker movement begun by Dorothy Day became popular destinations for placing clients. Dorothy had a shelter for the homeless in Tivoli, New York, and would accept anyone I drove down there with a warm welcome. I made one trip with a station wagon full of men. One of them was smoking and was so intoxicated that he lit himself on fire didn't even feel the pain. It destroyed my station wagon and I had to get help from friends to get back home.

An Albany Catholic woman named Mabel Gil, who was a good friend, had close ties to the Catholic Worker movement and was very committed to Dorothy Day's ministry. Mabel wrote legislation for the agricultural committee of the New York State Assembly that allowed local farms to sell their products to New York State institutions. Before that legislation, publicly funded institutions had to buy products only from larger companies that met certain codes that had been promoted by lobbyists. Another one of Mabel's bills created community gardens. Even today, as I drive around the state, I enjoy seeing all of the city folks who benefit from the experience of growing food in community gardens.

Another program that would accept even the most difficult homeless people was an outstanding project run by the Graymoor Friars in Ossining, New York. They were very much in touch with the needs of the addicted. I would load up our station wagon with folks who needed time away to try a sober lifestyle without any pressure from those who would arrest them for drinking.

Internal Debates

One of my many ministries at the time was serving as Chaplain to the Albany County Jail. There, I met many people who needed a powerful voice, so it was not beyond me to call Bishop Maginn for help. In the 1960s, the bishop was among the most influential people in the city, and he wasn't afraid to dive headlong into controversy.

For instance, a man named George Bunch had been arrested for inciting a riot and was in jail awaiting trial. Despite an outburst of anger in court, I advocated for him because I thought that he had mental health issues and needed help. I asked Bishop Maginn to visit him, which he did, and the local press covered it. Sadly, the visit annoyed many Albany residents, and the radio and media outlets were openly critical of the bishop. I thought he showed commitment to the poor and mentally ill who needed a voice in defense of their difficult plight.

This situation personified internal debates that were going on within the church, with priests and nuns claiming that church authority violated their personal freedom. Ordinations declined and priests were resigning from active ministry in the angry mid-1960s. Consequently, religious vocations were only 25 percent of what they were just five years prior. These "adjustment years" created confusion within our church community, but Bishop Maginn will always be my hero.

PART III
Advocating for Alcoholism Reform

Hospitals and Addiction

After many attempts, I failed to get addiction treatment accepted as a health issue. Not knowing what to do next, I met with Governor Rockefeller, and in due time the "Bureau of Alcohol Services" was formed with an office at 44 Holland Avenue in Albany.

A large number of New Yorkers, local agencies and medical personnel resisted the idea of recognizing addiction as a disease. The denial of medical care was common in the 1960s, and I brought many people back to our shelter to administer honey or orange juice for delirium tremors. Others died in my arms. To secure a bed or other medical assistance for our clients, I would sometimes offer a diagnosis that might qualify them for coverage by public or private insurance.

I finally worked out an agreement with four hospitals—Stratton Veterans Administration Hospital, Memorial Hospital, Albany Medical Center and St. Peter's Hospital. Each facility would accept one patient per night, but they needed to be paid. I had to provide a diagnosis of pancreatic disease, liver cirrhosis, nervous disorder or gastric problems in order to obtain insurance reimbursement.

Hospital staff resented the nightly referrals, but the Hughes Federal Act of 1970 threatened to take funding away from them if they denied parity of service to alcohol-related patients. Our clients' reputation for being disruptive frequently prompted the emergency room staff to put them in an area where their poor behavior would not cause distractions and prevent them from receiving care. At Albany Medical Center, our parish staff was told to always have someone available to babysit the folks we brought in, because some hospital staff thought it was a waste of time to care for these "bums." I gradually broke down their resistance after winning a sizeable grant to start an outpatient program at Albany Med, working with our Albany Citizens Council on Alcoholism.

The council was conceived in 1966 after I spoke at a policemen's breakfast. My talk served as a catalyst to bring individuals from various disciplines together to work on the problem of alcoholism. Mayor Corning was at the meeting and actively encouraged the development of an alcoholism program that would serve Albany. In January of 1968, the council announced the opening of an Alcoholism Information and Referral Center located in the Albany County Public Health Building at the corner of Green and South Ferry streets. Within a year, we had served 212 clients and processed 92 individuals for entry into rehabilitation facilities.

Our council clinic was the first in the United States to work with employee assistance treatment. In the Albany area, we tried to provide wellness services to more than 30,000 state workers, but because of their concerns about confidentiality, very few participated in the program. We then opened up the clinic to the whole community, and it became a big success; it remained open until the grant ended. Albany Med had located the program next to its morgue. We later moved it to our own site in an old public school on Madison Avenue, near Lark Street.

Holistic Treatment

My work with people addicted to alcohol and drugs made me aware that they struggle with a craving that emanates from the mesolimbic area of the brain—an area that affects thinking and decision-making. This is why we need to treat the addicted in a holistic manner. We cannot just detox addicts to get them through physical withdrawal and stop there.

Addicts need tools to help them understand their disease, and networking to help them rebuild their lives. They need aftercare treatment for a sustainable recovery and the dignity of a paycheck. These insights would later become the basis for our "three-legged stool" program. They would also lead to our pleading with local health authorities for assistance, but a common response at the time was that alcoholics were bums, vagrants and people who didn't want to help themselves. They were frequently harassed by local police and sent to jail. I saw the good in these folks, who didn't have any control over their compulsion to use mood-changing substances.

For example, I was in the shelter kitchen one night supervising our long lines of hungry clients. Apparently, a van driver began wrestling with one of the intoxicated men at the entrance to our gym. I never noticed the scuffle, and it was never reported to local police or any of our staff. A few months later, a lawyer seeking a settlement for the van driver, who claimed he was traumatically affected by the confrontation and lost his job as a result, contacted me. You just never knew what kind of person or problem would come through the door and the unexpected behavior that might follow.

Every night, I would walk among the people sleeping on cots or mats and turn each one on their side or stomach. Sadly, many were so severely intoxicated, I feared they might vomit and choke to death.

If someone couldn't sleep or was so drunk that he or she needed observation, we would bring that person to the front of the gym to talk with one of our 12-step volunteers, who would offer words of encouragement. Every night, I would make trips to the hospital with people in withdrawal.

The hospitals would accept many of our clients at this point, because we had gotten them through the most difficult days and they were generally pretty sober and stable. Finally, they would be in a therapeutic setting where they received the medical help they needed. We would try to put them in touch with their families, employers and any other positive support systems we could find.

At first, we would contact local restaurants for food and support. Siena College and the Stratton Veterans Administration Hospital donated our bedding. Many local farmers gave us permission to send some of our stronger men to their farms to harvest vegetables and other foods and bring them home.

I went to police court every day to gather up men who chose to come to our shelters rather than go to jail. I met many lawyers waiting for cases to appear on the docket, and several of them became most helpful to our work and allies for me. I kept repeating to anyone who would listen: "Treat, don't incarcerate." I spent so much time at police court, I was asked to become the court chaplain.

I attempted to change the public perception of our clients and community. One of our volunteers was Bob Danzig, publisher of the *Times Union* newspaper. At my request, Bob assigned Jean Arnold to cover us, and she was perfect for the job. She attended our meetings and wrote about good things that were happening, not just the negative crime reports from police court. We trusted Jean to be fair.

Negative stories in the media about our Black community impaired the needed progress of these great people who I knew firsthand. I recall visiting Al Hunter's family on Plum Street. While the adults enjoyed some sweet potato pie in the kitchen, we suddenly heard their children screaming the living room. Turns out they were screams of excitement. For the first time, they had seen a Black family on television being positively portrayed.

Sister Ignatia and Rosary Hall

Two friends of Bill Wilson, one of the co-founders of Alcoholics Anonymous, invited me to travel to Ohio for a close-up look at the organization in action. I was quick to say yes!

At the end of the school year in 1963, I left to go meet with Sister Mary Ignatia Gavin, CSA, at Rosary Hall in Cleveland's St. Vincent Charity Hospital. She had previously started a five-day recovery program at St. Thomas Hospital in Akron, Ohio, in 1939. It was Dr. Bob Smith himself, the other co-founder of AA, who had approached Sister Ignatia for help in getting a treatment program started at St. Thomas

The cost for a day of treatment at Rosary Hall back then was about $10 to $15. Sister Ignatia was insightful enough to label it "treatment," specifying that there was no cure for alcoholism. Sponsors were always working in the ward and anyone brought in had to express a sincere desire to participate in the 12-step program. The routine was demanding, especially for those who had only been there for a couple of days before being pressed into service to keep things organized.

Sister Ignatia would try to meet with the men on their final day and ask them to accept a Sacred Heart medallion. The patients treasured these medallions. They were the precursor to the "recovery coins" that are still passed out at AA meetings to this day. These simple gifts became an anniversary reminder for people who had made a commitment to sobriety.

While visiting Rosary Hall in July 1963, I met Father John McCarthy, who worked with the program. Sister Ignatia told me to follow him around to pick up some ideas. I wanted to collect all of their materials so I would have resources to help me jump-start our Albany detoxification program. I ended up staying with Father McCarthy because Sister Ignatia was not feeling well during my visit.

Bill Wilson and some other AA veterans would stop in to help Sister Ignatia prepare for retirement. She was worried that the disease model would be watered down to a "mental health" issue in order to obtain federal funding. It's amazing how she foresaw some of the difficulties that have indeed come to pass in most states. Alcoholism was relegated to a psychotic disorder, and that was where the law allocated public monies.

Armed with the materials that I had obtained in Ohio, I put my ideas into action. I incorporated the documents into a proposal and presented it to the St. Peters Hospital Board of Directors. I explained that the new program would include AA sponsorships, with the assigned readings, AA slogans and the roles patients would need to accept, all under the auspices of treatment. The program would emphasize taking a moral inventory of oneself and resolving not to take the first drink. Clients would be asked to let go of the past, to make amends to those they had offended and to develop a plan for outside sobriety.

After getting the new law passed that replaced incarceration with treatment, I selected St. Peter's Hospital to receive the funding. It provided $1.5 million to start-up programs for addiction services and, as parish pastor at our center, I allocated the money to begin a detox program. The hospital would have the authority to administer the proposed detox center, which would also provide addiction counseling. I consulted with St. Peter's CEO Sister Ellen Lawlor, RSM, and we decided to install a door to separate physical health services (supervised by the health department) from mental health services, which made state authorities happy and was a "first" for New York.

The addiction program was on the seventh floor of the Cusack Building at St. Peter's and later moved to the main hospital building. However, the individual lines of supervision caused confusion for local providers and, especially, for individuals seeking assistance with their disease. Little did I realize we were creating such a problem. Since then, I've attempted to implement holistic health programs that provide both physical and behavioral services.

There were a number of other 12-step type programs operating during this same time period. Many nights, I would take people with a need for withdrawal-supervised detoxification up to Betty Snyder's place in Saratoga Springs. The use of Antabus, a drug that produces unpleasant feelings in the body when combined with alcohol consumption, was popular with Betty. You could smell it as soon as you walked in the door.

I would also deliver clients, mostly women, to Margaret and Mickey McPike's old farmhouse on Route 67 in Ballston Spa. Women at the time were often terrified to be seen as criminals due to their drinking behavior, so they became closet drinkers who didn't reach out for help. As a result, they had no aftercare support or the housing that was needed to create a sober and supportive environment.

Margaret was a licensed practical nurse who worked with several local physicians. She had a knack for guiding women back into meaningful recovery through AA meetings, AA sponsorships and by playing recovery tapes by "Father John Doe." I later named a treatment center in Utica after her. Funded with help from State Senators Warren Anderson and Joe Pisani, it was one of 11 alcohol treatment centers that Governor Rockefeller allowed me to establish in preparation for new laws that would replace incarceration with treatment. The governor agreed that we needed to start with housing, and pledged to sign the law in 10 years while challenging me to pave the way equipped with one bill a year. When the time came, Governor Rockefeller was vice president of the United States and called to ask Gov. Malcolm Wilson to sign the new law.

I had previously brought many clients to Dick Caron's Chit Chat Farm in Pennsylvania, where a client would have about a month of recovery time. Dick became a great friend, guiding me toward many new ideas and instilling in me the need for a cooperative effort among the many leaders in the field. We would meet in the New York City AA Office of General Services with Marty Mann, the "first lady of AA," who also led the National Council on Alcoholism. She encouraged me to start a New York State council on alcoholism and to network with her good work in the national cause.

Dick Caron wanted me to start a rehabilitation program in the Albany area. "You've driven more than 100 clients to Wernersville (Pennsylvania) in just one year, and that proves that they need a rehab facility," he said. I approached Bishop William Scully to ask if it might be possible to start a Chit Chat program in Albany, but the bishop told me my active ministry in the South End required my complete dedication.

The debate about how to best help the addicted hasn't changed in 60 years, waged between programs that promote self-help and those that are professionally directed by funded resources. Now they operate in cooperation with one another, with recovering staff in supportive roles.

After 50 years in the field, I've heard all of the arguments about different forms of recovery treatment. I continue to believe the AA tradition of "attraction versus promotion:" persons in recovery can share their experience, strength and hope with others. Every day, I chat with people I meet to encourage them to accept help. I'm also aware of the concerns of clients who are forced into treatment, and of what has been accomplished with experienced "wounded healer" staff.

Some of My Role Models

I went to an open General Electric event in 1959 to meet Father Ralph Pfau at the International Union of Electrical Workers Hall in Schenectady and boy, it was a highlight for me. In 1949, Father Pfau had been the pioneer who convened Catholic clergy to pull together some priorities they thought needed to be addressed by our American Church. He was also known as Father John Doe. He had noticed a copy of the *Alcoholics Anonymous Big Book* on someone's shelf, borrowed it and consequently stopped drinking. His retreats were attended by thousands of Catholics and by many more thousands of non-Catholics.

His talks were eventually published and he founded the National Clergy Conference on Alcoholism, an organization devoted to the problems of priests that he directed for many years. Its publications, especially *Alcoholism: A Source Book for the Priest* and the annual *Blue Book*, made a deep impact on the American Catholic hierarchy.

Meeting him and hearing him speak was a treat. He used a little toy duck to illustrate compulsive drinking. Once it got wet, he held it in front of the microphone, and it continued to dip back into the glass for over an hour. I used the toy duck routine whenever I went to speak at high schools, and it always got the point of compulsive addiction across to students.

I admired so many of the early leaders; whenever I had a chance to meet them, I did. I needed their insights on some of the things I was attempting to do in the City of Albany. I was especially grateful for the discussions I had with Father John Ford, SJ, a respected Catholic theologian I quoted frequently. At the time, I was being challenged as to why I was wasting my time with "all of those bums." Even by the chancery, which frequently reminded me that I was assigned to the parish. My response was, "These are my parish members."

Father Ford, who applied Catholic moral theology to addiction, published Depth Psychology, Morality and Alcoholism. Mary C. Dara, an Alcoholics Anonymous historian, referred to Father Ford as "the first prominent Catholic theologian to speak out on the morality of alcohol use." She called him a "pioneer" in helping to prevent alcoholism through education. He argued that alcoholism should be defined as a disease and believed that it weakened individual sovereignty and responsibility. His point of view inspired modern pastoral approaches.

I was amazed how easy it was to talk to Father Ford about understanding the culpability of addiction. He defended the people who were supporting my efforts to decriminalize alcoholism. I appreciated having him just a telephone call away.

I also met with Fr. Joe Martin who produced great video programs that became very popular. I traveled with him, sharing his message, mostly in the many jails and prisons.

Legal Aid

The leadership of my own Catholic Church brought about many changes in my ministry. The biggest one came in the form of a visit by our diocesan attorney, Charles Tobin. He came to see the programs we had established on Green Street in 1962 to deal with the homeless and hundreds of others who were drinking and in need of treatment. Because of our clients' seizures, delirium tremors and other medical needs, he concluded that this type of operation was an insurance liability for the diocese. He suggested that if I wanted to continue to do this, I'd need to do it through my own nonprofit agency.

I was befriended by two attorneys who frequently defended clients of ours in trouble because of drinking. These noteworthy volunteers, John Devine and Frank Gavin, changed my life because I saw in them a special commitment to do their best to help the neediest of clients. It was a marriage of convenience for all of us. They were in recovery themselves and volunteered in our programs. They defended men who I saw almost every day in the soup kitchen at St. John's or in our shelter, sleeping on the old gym floor. This exchange of services created a wonderful team and became a learning experience for me. They showed me how I could better assist alcoholics.

These good folks would accompany me on many calls, not only men who were problem drinkers, but women who were in trouble as well. Many came from the AA clubhouse on lower Clinton Avenue, which allied with our efforts to assist problem drinkers.

We needed to show the state that our program provided a net savings by keeping clients out of the system. Even the sandwich given to someone in police custody, transportation to court and court costs add up. Placing people in an alternative program to incarceration is the best way. For many, it is the addiction that leads to the crime, and a legal mandate to programs like ours will keep them on a corrective path of recovery. This became "our product," an alternative that most counties would be happy to fund.

Our services kept folks out of the criminal justice system, which proved that our mission to provide employment and "create taxpayers" had been accomplished. Our agency staff dealt with the most difficult clients, according to national statistics, with amazing success. These people gained skills for their recovery and independence, along with the dignity of a paycheck. By many government and educational evaluations, we were proven to have saved millions of dollars in several parts of New York State, a major win for all taxpayers.

There's a popular saying understood by persons in 12-step recovery groups: "Did they hit their bottom?" People fall down the ladder by losing their relationship in a family, their home, their job and, eventually, their friends. The loss of each could be their bottom, and the ladder has to be rebuilt one rung at a time. Unfortunately, the ability to take those necessary, positive steps is often determined by one's health insurance coverage.

Alcohol addiction is a progressive, insidious disease. People build up a tolerance, and addiction controls them. In our shelter, I would give cots to those who had been sober for a few days as a reward and separate them from the "first-nighters" who, more times than not, exhibited boisterous behavior. I eventually got the "one-week-off-the-bottle" gang to help handle the hassles in the evening. I would reward them with a small job, driving them to the parish cemetery to help with the never-ending work of painting the fences or mowing the lawn. I would give them a little spending money so they could pick up some clean clothes. More importantly, it gave them the dignity of being able to say they had a job.

I maintained a close relationship with a YMCA next to the train station, where people with Social Services benefits could be housed for $2.75 and $3.15 a night. Moving clients there from a shelter not only provided better accommodations, it also entitled them to a clothing allowance given to people in certified occupancy rooms.

Photographed here with his mother Eleanor, Father Young won the "Beautiful Baby of the Year" contest sponsored by Sears Roebuck. Father in front of the Eleanor Young Outpatient Clinic (below) named in her honor.

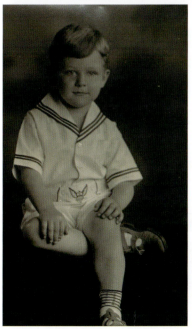

Left: Father at 3 years old. Right: Dressed for his first day of school at St. Teresa's in Albany, NY.

Left: Father attended Christian Brothers Academy (CBA) in Albany.
Below: Proof that even legends get into trouble sometimes... Father's CBA demerit for having dirty shoes.

At Christian Brothers Academy, Father played baseball, football and basketball. (Father is pictured in the top row, at far right.) He attended Siena College after playing baseball with the Negro Leagues as a teen.

My Life's Journey

While playing for Siena's baseball team, Father was injured so badly in a game against Utica that he wound up bedridden and in rehab for over a year.

PETE YOUNG—Siena first baseman, injured in the Utica game will probably be sidelined for the St. Michael's game.

In 1953, Father was drafted by the Navy, causing him to miss tryouts with the St. Louis Cardinals baseball team. During his tour of duty, the ship's captain was so impressed by Peter's gift for making a difference in people's lives, he urged him to become a priest.

Father as a Semanarian at St. Bonaventure.

Left: Father's Ordination in May 1959 with his mother Eleanor and father Pete, Senior. Below: Father blessing his grandmother after ordination.

Father Young's formal ordination portrait.

Father developed the PYHIT concept of the three-legged stool model for recovery in the 1960s. Right: Chatting with program volunteers.

Left: Father was named pastor of St. John's Church in the South End of Albany and became known as a "street priest." Pictured here in 1975 with parishioner Mabel Gill.

By the 1980s, Father had started what became Peter Young Housing, Industries and Treatment (PYHIT). At its apex, Peter Young Housing had 117 programs from Brooklyn to Buffalo. Left: Father in front of the Altamont House.

Father Young (left) with baseball legend Stan Musial (middle) who played with the St. Louis Cardinals for 22 seasons en route to the Hall of Fame. The identity of the other gentleman is unknown.

Left to right: Bob Ward, PYHIT Board President; Albany Mayor Jerry Jennings; Tyler Trice, President of the Ida Yarborough Tenants Association; and Father Young.

Father with two PYHIT board members in the 1980s: Kevin Luibrand, Father's cousin (left), and George Schindler (right), who also served as president of the program's housing entity.

Father urged recovering addicts to channel pain into helping others by being "wounded healers" who could lead AA meetings and counsel others.

Left: Father conducting a group session at the Eleanor Young Outpatient Clinic.

Right: Conversing with residents at 37 South Ferry Street in Albany, New York.

Father outside of a program-run mini-mart on North Pearl Street in Albany. He's joined by PYHIT Chief Operating Officer Jackie Gentile and store manager Alvin Fernandez.

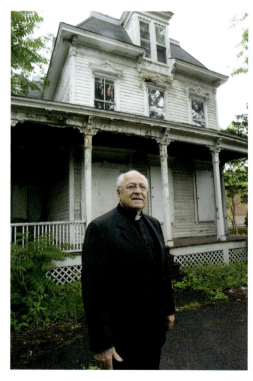

Father scouting properties for possible use by PYHIT programs.

Father on a neighborhood walk meeting and greeting PYHIT clients and staff along Ferry and Green streets in Albany's South End.

Father shares a smile with students and workers in the PYHIT Culinary Arts Program at the Schuyler Inn in Menands, NY.

Father in the State Capitol where he was Chaplain of the New York State Senate for years. He knew everyone in state government from the governors on down, which was essential to obtaining grant and member items to support the PYHIT programs.

Two legends together: Father with NFL Hall-of-Famer Jim Brown at an event in 2004.

Father and Director of Parole Stabilized Residents Michael Westbrook on South Ferry Street in Albany. Father's first parish, St. John's, is in the background.

Above: Father with New York State Senator Joe Bruno. Left: Attending an annual legislative dinner with Congressman Mike McNulty. Below: Father with Lieutenant Governor Kathy Hochul and Assemblywoman Pat Fahey in 2015.

Left to right: Albany Bishop Howard Hubbard, PYHIT Chief Operating Officer Jackie Gentile and Father Peter G. Young.

Father and his mother Eleanor in the 1980s at the Blessed Sacrament Church in Bolton Landing, NY.

Father and his mother Eleanor with two parishioners in Bolton Landing.

Father at the Schuyler Inn in Menands, NY, with friends Dick Terlingen (left) and Larry Sheffield (right).

An original antique birch canoe from Fort Ticonderoga served as the altar for special events during Father's ministry at the Blessed Sacrament Parish in Bolton Landing, NY.

The canoe was gifted to Father when he left Bolton. Here it is strapped to his car for the trip down the Northway. With him are parishioners Kathy Spahn (middle) and Donna Langan.

Children help Father Young celebrate his birthday in 2015 at Mother Teresa's Rectory on Second Avenue in Albany.

Father celebrates his 90th Birthday with friends.

Every summer for more than 20 years, hundreds of supporters have gathered at a gala hosted by Saratoga National Golf Club in Saratoga Springs, NY, to raise money for the Peter G. Young Foundation.

Father flanked by longtime friends and supporters Tom Newkirk (left), President and CEO of Saratoga National Golf Club, and Peter Newkirk (right), a former PYHIT Volunteer CEO.

After his retirement, Father remained involved in PYHIT as a volunteer and said Mass daily in a chapel in the basement of Albany's Picotte Building on Washington Avenue.

Father working on his autobiography in his backyard.

Guests in our gym did not qualify because we were not a certified place of occupancy. We had several battles with the New York State Department of Social Services over this.

I was always grateful for the work of Dr. C. Carlyle Nuckols Jr., the state Social Services commissioner, who took an interest in this matter. Some counties refused to cooperate with our out-of-county referrals, but Dr. Nuckols set up a system enabling me to submit a form filled out by our parish shelter coordinator on behalf of the client, and Social Services would pay the counties directly out of the New York State Social Services budget. This was a great help because, although the state would not fund our shelters, they would fund a residential housing program. This gave me about $2.00 a day to house and feed one client. With that, I was able to raise enough money to get a residential program off the ground.

New York has always been a block grant-funded state that prevents benefits from being awarded to those who do not have documented housing. When those clients apply, they are assigned a pending status. It takes many months to find out whether they will be sponsored by the agency from which they are receiving services. Too often, an agency has already provided services when it finds out that the client has not been approved. This results in a denial of anticipated payments, a cost borne by the agency. Frequently, smaller counties also do not have the needed programs. Their residents go to a catchment area that has services, which denies their application for aid.

Many agencies like ours found it difficult to serve the needy population. We lost more than a million dollars a year serving clients who sincerely wanted to recover but did not have the money to pay for help. We operated under the ideal that "if you have a desire to stop using, then we give you a program." However, giving away free care got us in trouble. When we had empty beds, we accepted people into our program—many from prison and homeless sites. Often, a judge would mandate a bed assignment and our agency would accept them, even in "pending" status, only to find out later that their treatment was denied.

PART IV
Albany and Racial Equality in the 1970s

Migration from the South

In the mid-1970s, there were hundreds of new families from the South coming to Albany. But those in control of Albany politics did not allow any opportunities for the new arrivals who went to the county for assistance. Most of these folks from the troubled South held to the American dream of equal rights and receiving some help during this period of desegregation, but it wasn't possible for them to find employment. It was a difficult economy and newcomers just did not have the necessary connections.

One of the more important issues from the early 1960s still festered beneath the surface in the Black community: the anger Black men felt about not being able to find decent employment. They considered this a form of racism. For example, we had a Parent-Teacher Association at our parish school of 280 students, most of whom were Black. Only one father was listed as a parent among all of our PTA members.

For these men, jobs were limited to cleaning, working at a brickyard, serving as porters or picking fruit in season. Civil service jobs and union memberships were just not available to them. Therefore, we existed in a matriarchal society in the South End, with men unable to find sufficient work to support their families.

The welfare agency would send out what we called "midnight raiders," officials sent to visit homes to try to catch men living with their families, thereby disqualifying them from receiving public assistance. The men would be forced to appear in court for failure to support their children. Many of our efforts began to center on finding job opportunities for the men.

We started our own employment agency at St. John's, and it became a major priority for many years. We had volunteers, many retired from state jobs, who would help Black men prepare resumes and even drive them around for job interviews. In one year, Bill Murray, a volunteer who worked at the state Education Department, by himself was able to get 741 men respectable full-time positions.

Regardless how menial a city job might be, applicants had to be approved by Chairman Leo Quinn in the Democratic Party office at 11 North Pearl Street. While Dan O'Connell did not hold an elected office, there was never any doubt that he was at the helm in the City and County of Albany. Their leaders willingly helped as best they could with many part-time positions.

Playing Politics

Albany Mayor Erastus Corning 2nd was a well-established man from a deep-rooted, powerful, wealthy family. Working with Democratic Chairman O'Connell, Mayor Corning did his job so well, he became Albany's longest-serving mayor (1942-1986). The Albany political machine outlasted even the powerful Daley family in Chicago. Governor Thomas Dewey (1942-1954) attempted to lodge an investigation of O'Connell and Corning, but it was unsuccessful and they emerged unscathed.

Mayor Corning was a fascinating politician. He was always

available. One could head over to his office and get a meeting immediately to discuss any concerns. He would give a quick "yes" or "no" without the need for committees or paperwork. He told people exactly how he felt, expressed in both words and deeds.

Migrants from the South put pressure on the Social Services system, which led to many a confrontation with the Corning administration. An example that comes to mind is our attempt to provide free health services to South End residents.

St. John's parish had the support of the St. Luke's Physicians Guild, led by Jack Grogan, MD. The guild provided doctors who volunteered three nights a week in our medical clinic at 35 South Ferry Street. People might come in to get a simple physical for a job or school, or for some insurance matter. The clinic went over very well with the community and its success was reported in a local newspaper. This embarrassed the mayor because volunteers were doing the work and the idea wasn't initiated by the city. So, Mayor Corning sent a code officer to check our clinic for possible violations. Corning himself paid a visit and declared that the lighting was inadequate. As a result, the free clinic was closed.

There was a strong backlash to the closing from local residents. The mayor responded by calling a press conference to announce that the county would build a new state-of-the-art Department of Health building across the street at 175 Green. He thanked me for starting a good program and said the county would improve upon the services offered. This seems to me like a good illustration of the old adage "losing the battle but winning the war." The people benefitted from a better health care system while the mayor shook hands with and thanked our volunteers.

The lesson I learned was that the city administration wanted to control all services provided to the people. Thereafter, whenever I saw a need, I demonstrated it by instigating some related activity and the city would respond with funding.

Governor Nelson A. Rockefeller nominated me to several federal positions representing New York State, which allowed me to hear about upcoming grant opportunities. I always tried to secure those grants for the City of Albany.

I recall unintentionally encroaching on Mayor Corning's turf on one occasion when I tried to provide some summer programs for our youth. South Enders had little going on during the summer months, so I went down to Washington to secure funding for a summer camp for kids. We opened up the program on the Lawson Lake campgrounds in Feura Bush, but the city quickly stepped in and said it would be operating the summer program the following year. I actually felt great about that, because I had just received a three-year grant for the program. In fact, the summer program at Lawson Lake has continued to this day and enjoys strong community support.

Some local politicians thought I might run for office. An independent newspaper reported this rumor, which got me in trouble. People started calling me, eager to fund my "campaign." Soon after that information reached Dan O'Connell and Mayor Corning, I had to obtain permits every time I needed to use a baseball field or a park for our youth programs. Previously, use of these facilities had always been free and open to the public. Now I needed the mayor's signature for every game, and I had to talk for hours with the mayor's office to obtain it. Now, virtually anything I wanted to do in the city depended upon their approval. The mayor would still arrange a photo op, with a smile on his face, to announce events planned for the South End… but city code officers were always waiting in the wings.

As Governor Rockefeller's appointee to federal health committees under the Kennedy and Johnson administrations, I had successfully written a federal grant application that provided our center with funding to create an expanded city youth recreation program. The mayor preferred to transfer the administration of the grant to his office so he could appoint the staff.

PART V
Learning the Ropes of Legislation

Governor Rockefeller

Living only minutes from the State Capitol, I went there frequently to lay the groundwork for improving the lives of the people who kept coming to our parish and programs. I would ask anyone and everyone in state government to listen. Senator Edward Speno (R-Nassau County) became my greatest ally. My childhood friend Harry Albright, appointments secretary to Governor Rockefeller, provided me access with an invitation for a friendly cup of coffee.

The years up through 1974 were a dreamtime for me. The governor suggested I be named chaplain at the state Senate. We would talk about legislation whose passage might be needed, rather than reading all the lobbyists' research documents. I often think he might have preferred discussions because of his dyslexia.

A close, trusted relationship with Governor Rockefeller and his staff gave us new laws that benefited the inner city, criminal justice and, most of all, the addicted homeless. The governor visited St. John's and saw the real South End, which opened his mind about our supportive programs. Usually, high-level political leaders are led around when they visit facilities, which means they only see the best and not the reality. But the governor saw our overcrowded gym, where people didn't pay attention to his title, and would question him. One of our own, Olivia, said to him, "Listen, honey, you need to do something to help us." It was amazing to watch the governor listen carefully to regular folks—people he normally wouldn't meet one-on-one without the press covering it.

Just as a side note, the governor's relaxed demeanor was one reason the riot at the Attica prison on Sept. 9, 1971, confused me. He didn't go to meet with the 2,200 inmates and their leaders during the four-day conflict, in which 10 staff and 33 inmates were killed. I believe, with his skill for talking out problems, his presence would have resolved the standoff.

Networking for Legislative Reform

As a parish priest trying to make inroads with state leaders, I tried to leverage any opportunity I could find that might open up doors for the needy youth and adults we were attempting to serve. Maintaining a presence in all types of associations and on boards served my strategy of building a power base so that these issues could eventually be recognized. I volunteered to do whatever public policy committee work I could find. But being a member of the clergy did not always benefit our efforts. Many legislators considered me a "do-gooder" and certainly not one with a constituency.

Still, my networking with state agencies began to open doors, as did my mother's friendships with people in positions to influence those with power. Mom was involved in many different associations and had local political relationships. At the time, she held a job in the office of New York State Comptroller Arthur Levitt. One day, he came to her desk and said, "Eleanor, a little more work and a little less entertaining!" Nevertheless, she knew power brokers, several of whom made calls to the comptroller. It was not long before mom was told to relax and continue her welcoming manner with all who came to his office. He never corrected her again, and he became a great friend of the family.

Many friends in the Albany area continued to support me by encouraging people in key positions to hear me out. But it was the introduction to Governor Rockefeller by Harry Albright that gave me the foundation for finally getting real results. The governor even assigned me a parking spot on the Capitol ramp next to his limousine. Many good things began to happen because of such friendships. If a State Assembly member needed Senate support for a proposed house bill, I became their connection.

One of the many difficulties legislators encounter is dealing with party differences. If someone sits on one side of the aisle, he or she is expected to vote against proposals presented by the other side of the aisle. This resulted in the failure to pass many bills that would have done much for the public good. Well-minded folk from low-level staff would tell me that proposed legislation was ignored by the majority leaders in their respective houses unless there was a public outcry. I was able to quietly take some bills from one side of the aisle to the other, suggesting endorsement.

The result in many cases was the passage of a bill that benefited the citizenry. For example, the bill that created community gardens had at first been put in the "dead" file. I quietly gave it to a friend in the other house, asking for sponsorship, and it eventually passed both legislative branches. I was pleased to have had a hand in legislation that encouraged institutions in New York State to buy from local farmers. The bill created a direct purchasing market for local, fresher products at lower prices for all.

I achieved results by facilitating bipartisanship. Being around the Capitol for so many years enabled me to gain the confidence of legislators from both sides of the aisle.

Bills and Support

The Urban Education Bill was something I was very interested in because it would provide about $63 million in funding for inner-city schools from Brooklyn to Buffalo. The speaker of the New York State Senate, Senator Earl Bridges (R-Majority Leader, 1966-72), was always receptive and most of his staff were eager to assist. His chief of staff, George Heim, who was there for almost 50 years, was a close friend of my mother's and got me through many doors where I could support the bill. However, it never passed.

St. John's School, with its 95% minority and only 15% Catholic student body, caught the eye of Governor Rockefeller. He asked if he could come to visit with Senator Bridges and hold a town hall-style meeting in our gym, at which time he would announce agreement on the bill.

One of the difficulties I had at this time was acquiring the support of the Public Policy Committee of the New York State Catholic Conference. The legal staff of the conference questioned my efforts at the Capitol and their lack of advocacy on behalf of the inner city upset me.

While the Urban Education Bill was being proposed, the Public Policy Committee was supporting another piece of legislation—the Speno-Lerner Bill. This proposal offered broader support for schools, including the state's Catholic schools. The Catholic Conference was lobbying for it and saw my attempt to get the Urban Education Bill passed as problematic.

We had many difficult meetings with attorney Charles Tobin, who was representing the state's bishops. Ultimately, I was told by him to back off, and the Catholic Conference told me to withdraw my support for the Urban Education Bill, as the broader bill had the support to pass. But the Speno-Lerner Bill did not make it through either house. The failure of the Urban Education Act became the precursor for what, 30 years later, would be the foundation of both for-profit and nonprofit charter schools.

I felt Governor Rockefeller would have had a winner with the Urban Education Bill. After it failed to pass, my problems with the Public Policy Committee continued. Because I had rallied support for the Urban Education Bill by visiting all of the inner-city parishes in New York's eight dioceses, I was looked upon with suspicion as a priest with a special agenda that was not in compliance with that of the conference.

An attempt to get legislation passed on behalf of inner city, non-public schools surfaced again in February 2009. The *New York Times* reported that Mayor Michael R. Bloomberg and Bishop Nicholas A. DiMarzio of the Diocese of Brooklyn unveiled a proposal to convert four Roman Catholic schools singled out for closure into public charter schools. The eleventh-hour lifeline was meant to preserve the education provided in these buildings and stave off potential overcrowding in city schools. The article claimed "it would be the first time such a plan was undertaken in New York and could serve as a model for converting other Catholic and private schools."

Despite tensions with the Catholic Conference, there were some benefits. As they became aware of our concerns, I was invited to join in on discussions about their monthly agenda. It was a chance to become involved with the bishops of New York State in a positive way, and it gave me a voice and a mechanism to work with them.

In frequent sessions with the bishops, I met many outstanding men. I usually sat next to Bishop Fulton J. Sheen, later made venerable by the church. If only my mother could have seen that! The meetings were held at the Sheraton Hotel at LaGuardia Airport in New York City. Being a baseball fan, I would usually receive an invitation to attend a Mets game with them after the meeting. My admiration of the bishops' dedication only grew stronger as I got to know them better.

Background on Bills

There are miles of archives at the Capitol containing data on legislation for which I advocated: proposals to promote education, new treatment centers, insurance, employee assistance, and criminal justice and parole programs. I checked on any bill that had the word "alcohol" in it. Would it lessen the penalties or increase them? Was there any language that made mention of alcoholism as a disease?

Often, when I would ask a senator to support the addicted, he would tell me, "Alcoholics don't vote for me; I only listen to those who do." That was my rationale for wandering around New York State to establish a widespread voice for our addiction constituency. I encouraged other community leaders to help by starting a state association of councils on alcoholism. I tried to organize representatives from many counties to move toward the goal of a unified state voice for treatment programs.

I adopted a new style that helped me avoid topics likely to trigger a defensive attitude from legislators. I wandered the halls and mixed with staff from both sides of the aisle, gradually asking for things that I know they would consider helpful for their constituents. I've joined legislators at many social gatherings and mixed with them as a friend. When I couldn't access them directly, I tried to build a trusting relationship with their staff, engaging in small talk.

Today, the leadership decides which bills are appropriate for consideration. The legislators are just the front line. Any suggestions for bills are now sent to the leaders for a final okay, then put on the calendar for a vote and if passed sent to the governor for signing. Legislators who are in danger of losing their seats get the best treatment from party leadership. They're given extra money for line items so they can build up some "stock" before it's time for re-election.

I was mistaken in thinking that just proposing good ideas would bring about results. I was deeply disappointed when I attended countless meetings without anything to show for my efforts. This was one of the most important lessons I learned.

I began to propose bills to the finance committee instead of the program committee. I learned that showing a positive financial outcome would make things happen. Legislators are always looking to demonstrate that proposed legislation will result in actual savings to their budgets and constituents.

I also learned that asking legislators for support on member items outside of their district was problematic. For example, when I attempted to decriminalize public intoxication, I found I had to establish a statewide network of councils on alcoholism that would include many legislators' districts. It took many years to find supportive leaders in all of the different parts of the state. And when I did, they were frequently grounded in the thinking of the temperance movement, believing that abstinence was the answer to alcoholism and that it was a moral issue.

Councils on Alcoholism: Up and Running

As the councils on alcoholism became a reality, the next step was trying to network them statewide. Many times established agencies would not allow our council members, most of whom were in recovery, to attend their meetings. It took a long time for agencies to accept people who admitted they had a problem in the past.

In my many years of meetings with Governor Rockefeller, he told me that he believed in what I was doing and was encouraged by our work. He said he would support decriminalizing public intoxication. One of the greatest experiences I ever had was when the governor provided me with a letter of endorsement that empowered me to go to 19 different state mental health campus locations and tell their directors to establish addiction rehabilitation sites for 40 to 60 patients. I felt like a kid in a candy store. All I needed to do was ask when and where on their campus and they would implement the program site.

The success I was enjoying started with a program to house certain drug offenders in Department of Correctional Services addiction recovery dorms. Court professionals signed up people who accepted the conditions of an intensive treatment program. This mental health model was eventually cancelled by the legislature due to its cost. Within a week, staff working as counselors were told to report to work in uniform as corrections officers.

Still, with the governor's letter, I felt like John the Baptist "preparing the way" for the signing of the law 10 years later that would decriminalize public intoxication.

The office of Bill Passannante, speaker pro tem of the Assembly, became a focal point for my work on behalf of the homeless and addicted. Bill was generous about helping people in need. We shared offices with many famous people from the New York City arts community who were seeking support for their cultural programs. Frequently, New York Mayor John Lindsay would speak with me about his days trying to calm race riots. On other occasions, I would chat with Mayor Abraham Beame of New York City or Kitty Carlisle

Hart, the actress and singer known for her appearances as a game show panelist. Bill would often bring me to New York City for meetings. He was a local hero among his constituents.

My first real breakthrough impacting legislation came with the assistance of Senator Edward Speno, chair of the Senate Finance Committee. I proposed that the philosophy of 12-step programs should be incorporated in our educational and correctional facilities. Senator Speno carefully listened and eventually made the recommendation to the New York State Department of Education. John Sinacore, who became director of education, set up new guidelines for the Bureau of Health Education. Unfortunately, he received little support for those efforts, and being the "new guy on the block," it wasn't easy for him. The bureau never received the full support it needed.

Senator Speno and I went on many trips to present the bureau's agenda. We found that strong, loyal, sensitive teachers in the field supported us. As I look back on this experience, I can see that we were 20 years ahead of our time. The program became part of the curriculum for grammar and high schools across the state, picking up speed because of growing public concern about drugs.

Block Grants

In order to understand how the money flows that supports our state programs and how it is distributed at the community level, one has to understand "formula" or "block grant" funding. Block grants are a type of mandatory grant awarded for specific types of work based on statistical criteria. The authorizing legislation and regulations outline the standards and the amount of funds to be distributed. The term "formula" refers to the way the funds are distributed to the recipient.

In contrast, a discretionary grant is one in which organizations (and sometimes individuals) submit applications for a competitive review and selection process. Block grants are non-competitive. Medicaid is an example of block grant funding.

New programs can be put into the state purpose budget as discretionary funding, which can be very quickly implemented (especially on state property, where there is no worry about building code or zoning problems).

In 1974, the administration of Governor Hugh Carey and Budget Director Peter Goldmark, who was originally from Boston, came up with the idea of integrating the matching federal and county share of funding into all local New York assistance budgets. This proved to be an outstanding lift to the state budget, saving 75 percent of the cost of federally funded Medicaid programs.

Medicaid had been assigned to the local Department of Social Services in 1966 because it was thought that localities knew best how to address poverty. (Thirty years later, it would be transferred to the State Department of Health.) The practice of shared state and local financing of non-federal program costs was designed to enable state financing of social welfare programs requiring a state match. Upstate counties embraced the practice because statewide Medicaid expenses at that time were expected to be approximately 70 percent of all costs.

In 2010, the state expanded its administrative oversight and responsibility for health policy and Medicaid with the passage of the Patient Protection and Affordable Care Act, also known as "Obamacare." At the same time, the state legislature mandated a five-year plan for the state to assume Medicaid administration. A larger state role in program management would be an important element of this effort.

The Hughes Comprehensive Alcohol Abuse and Alcoholism

Prevention, Treatment and Rehabilitation Act of 1970 had set new requirements for state planning incentives for hospitals to admit alcoholics, and for the confidentiality of records. The act gave states formula grants for the funding of community-based programs. The advent of block grant funding shifted the payment for services, which received support from a percentage of federal, state and county payments. Agencies would then set up rules and regulations to assure their clients had high quality of care.

From that time on, our private agencies would respond to a request for local discretionary funds and then be fined or convicted of a crime if the funds were not spent for the purpose approved. Shifting from assisting to compliance turned the agency's role from helping to that of policing.

United States Senator Harold Hughes and I were sent on national speaking tours to promote the concept of addiction as a disease. R. Brinkley Smithers, the recovering alcoholic and benefactor of many programs that addressed alcoholism, financed these tours. Smithers established the Christopher D. Smithers Foundation, a charitable organization that focused on alcoholism education and treatment. By the mid-1990s, his foundation and the Smithers family had donated more than $37 million to support alcoholism-related projects. In fact, Brinkley funded my trip to St. Louis in 1974 to debate Jerry Falwell. Falwell was a leading minister of the Southern Baptist clergy who claimed, in his own words, that alcoholism contradicted Christian morality. At that conference, his arguments were well received by those in attendance.

Senator Hughes, also a recovering alcoholic, was always full of great stories. Eight years older than me, he was an outstanding Democratic Senate leader and former governor of Iowa. I enjoyed working with him as an advocate for treatment. He would say,

"Treatment is virtually nonexistent because addiction is not recognized as an illness."

Assemblyman Julius Volker and, later, his son Dale also provided funds for treatment. State Senator Dale Volker would become a key sponsor and friend who would go with me to the gym after legislative sessions to play basketball. Working in the Senate, I was able to ignite the movement for the Councils on Alcoholism that provided resources for local advocates around the state to establish programs at the county level. Senator Lee Metcalf was a former housing director from Auburn, New York, who became a strong advocate for health programs, as did Senator Bill Conklin, who was a champion for anyone with a disability.

Some of the 1970 Senators who provided aid for the addicted were the newer members: Senators Basil Paterson (father of Governor David Paterson), and Senator Ron Stafford. They got it; they understood the needs of our addicted citizens.

Years later, Senator Stafford chaired the finance joint hearing and congratulated Commissioner Tom Coughlin for the addiction programs within the New York State Department of Corrections. The commissioner replied with anger about how funding for these programs was inserted into his budget by an "outsider." I was that outsider. It was my request to Senator Stafford that got the Alcohol and Substance Abuse Treatment program up and running. By asking for line items in Commissioner Coughlin's budget without any prior discussions, I would be thought of as denigrating him and his staff. I had to be humble, because just one item started the expansion of the recovery program throughout the correctional system.

In due time, Commissioner Coughlin congratulated me and offered me a superintendent's position. I figured that if I accepted, I would wind up on the Canadian border, far away from the legislators and unable to submit ideas to them. Later, when Tom retired, he and I spoke at a national mental health conference. We talked about opportunities for our clients in community reintegration over dinner and agreed to work together. Later that same week, I was shocked and sorry to hear that he had succumbed to a heart attack.

Capitol Battles

The heaviest and yet most satisfying battles that I have had at the Capitol were waged over the passage of major legislation that would reorganize the departments of Mental Health, the Developmentally Disabled, and Substance Abuse and Alcoholism. Senator Frank Padavan was a believer in the need for us to maintain our autonomous, disease-centered philosophy.

With the support of the Senate, I was given a strong hand to hold out for agreement on a $3.5 million budget. The Senate issued me a letter stating that, when I agreed, they would put the bill on the calendar for passage.

Led by Senator Joe Zaretzki, during an election cycle when Democrats had gained control of the Senate, we were able to obtain passage of his bill securing $2 million for our treatment programs.

Governor Malcolm Wilson (1973-74) was the most delightful person that I have ever met at the Capitol. He had knowledge of the system and it was with great joy that, when Governor Rockefeller left to become vice president, Malcolm Wilson became New York's governor. He called me in and, without any fanfare, said that he was encouraged by Governor Rockefeller to sign the bill on decriminalization. All of the people who wrote or lobbied to oppose decriminalization said that I had ruined the criminal justice system. One of the angriest opponents was Albany District Attorney John

Clyne, who at that time was coordinating the New York State District Attorneys' Association.

When Governor Wilson lost his bid for election to Hugh Carey in 1974, my work and world quickly changed. I lost all of my previous contacts at the Capitol, not to mention my parking spot next to the governor's. I no longer had any privileges or open doors at the agencies. I had suggested various bills for the creation of a Bureau of Alcoholism as part of the Department of Mental Health, but they did not want to hear it.

Governor Wilson had told me to talk about the proposed legislation with the state Department of Health, but that turned out to be a bust. Dr. Joe Robinson, the commissioner, was in charge of the public health division. He said the department felt the proposed legislation would be detrimental to its mission and would stigmatize its services. Eventually, it was assigned to the Executive Branch and then to the Department of Mental Health, but for many years the bureau was poorly funded at less than one percent of their budget.

When there's a change in state leadership, you have to begin to identify the people you can count on to advocate on behalf of your legislation. I would always attempt to maintain a strong friendship with a leading Democrat and a Republican in order to have them anchor any of the meetings or the bills that needed sponsorship. My favorite combination was Deputy Speaker Bill Passannante, a Democrat, and Senator Tom Laverne, a Republican. I would meet with them at least three times a week for dinner. Through their understanding and vision, great things came about.

A breakthrough happened in the 1970s. Governor Carey signed into law a bill mandating the reorganization of New York's Department of Mental Health. The bill created the Division of Alcoholism and Alcohol Abuse Services and granted autonomy to this new division.

In 1973, a national program called the Comprehensive Employment and Training Act, or CETA, was enacted to provide jobs for unemployed persons, including students. CETA provided a very important opportunity to help the needy around the state. I was honored to serve as the co-chair with A. Philip Randolph, who led Blacks and whites in the Brotherhood of Sleeping Car Porters and championed changes that ended discrimination in many industries. He was the founder of the first major Black union and the first vice president of the AFL-CIO, an office he held for more than a decade.

Randolph confronted President Franklin D. Roosevelt over segregation in the military. Roosevelt eventually issued an executive order that created a fair employment practices commission. Randolph also confronted President Harry Truman over racial segregation in the U.S. military and threatened that if segregation continued, he would urge young Black men to defy the draft. He admonished President John F. Kennedy who was trying to talk civil rights leaders out of holding the March on Washington. Randolph had organized the 1963 march, an event I assisted with, and he continued to be a respected leader until his death in 1979.

But there was a problem. It seemed that with every change of administration, the new guard wanted its name on the labor programs. So I was assigned to tell people employed in the CETA program throughout the state that the program was closing. I thanked them for serving, and at the same time told them there were no longer any public service job opportunities. I still remember the tears I encountered from a woman who approached me in Plattsburgh. She said her job was to clean the bathrooms in city hall, a menial task she had been doing for 10 years. "Why am I being fired?" she asked. I had no answer.

State of the State – 1973

The January 3, 1973, State of the State address delivered by Governor Rockefeller was a shocking experience for me. At that point in his political career, he was looking for support as he contemplated a run for president of the United States. He needed backing from the conservative right and was viewed by them and his GOP rivals as too liberal. In his eagerness to do something to win their confidence, he took aim at rehabilitation programs and blatantly stated, "This has to stop."

The governor proposed a mandatory sentence of life in prison for anyone convicted of selling heroin, methadone and various other drugs. Once passed, the legislation became known as the "Rockefeller Drug Laws."

I was deeply involved in many of the discussions, but when the governor's education team took over, they made all of the decisions and they were all politically motivated. For years afterward, our state correctional facilities were filled with people who had done little more than use marijuana. This became an extremely expensive mandate.

Finally, in 2009, we would get these laws repealed, giving sentencing discretion back to the judges. It was "rehabilitation versus incarceration." Let the punishment fit the crime and the individual case be considered, instead of a block of mandated sentences. Governor Paterson led all of these new progressive laws.

Thus began a conversation that was bothersome for me. In the field, a consensus that there was a difference between "soft" and "hard" drugs was beginning to surface. The government was aware of the crime problems associated with "hard drugs" like heroin and cocaine, while accepting the false notion that the "soft drug" marijuana was recreational. This became a focus and a major concern of political leaders in our country.

Attorney Keith Stroup, founder of the National Organization for the Reform of Marijuana Laws, led the campaign to decriminalize marijuana. A number of our clients said their drug addiction started with marijuana use. One thing leads to another in the addiction field, thus we were opposed to the legalization and decriminalization of this particular drug.

Finding Funding

Funding for alcohol rehabilitation did not come easy. In the mid-1970s, the New York State budget for drugs was more than a quarter of a billion dollars, and only $13 million of that was slated for alcohol-related services. Most of the state resources in these areas went to grants for agencies attempting to serve hard-core drug clients. Alcohol services agencies had to raise a good portion of their own money.

Our alcohol agencies were very involved with the fellowship of AA, but in a major conference orchestrated by Governor Carey, 90% of all addiction programs prioritized abstinence as the preferred approach to recovery. New York State became a battleground between the behavior modification model of the "therapeutic community" and 12-step programs. As the chairperson and founder of the New York State Council on Alcoholism, this philosophical difference totally consumed 10 years of my life. It required daily visits to the Capitol to defend our 12-step philosophy.

The treatment approaches proposed by both sides were very different. It was difficult being on the Governor's Council and writing a minority opposition opinion. As a member of the Governor's Advisory Committee opposing his proposed legislation, I had to stop the $3.5 million bill from being enacted. Warren Anderson sent me a letter stating that the Senate would put the bill to a vote only if my concerns were addressed. This put me on a collision course with a governor I deeply respected, but on this issue we totally disagreed. He did not understand the value of the fellowship program and the 90% majority of our New York State Council on Alcoholism constituency.

The logic of the time was to combine the two agencies' administrations to save money. I was called upon to change my position and support the establishment of the new combined agency. I was told how new computer systems would be better able to monitor the two agencies as one. The governor's staff and others said there would be problems, and the bishop was called and informed that I was preventing the bill from passing. The bishop said that I did not speak for the Catholic Church, but that I had a right as a citizen to express my opinions.

I left a letter on the governor's desk stating my concerns and nervously headed home. As soon as I arrived, I received a call. It was the governor. He said that if I could come to the Capitol immediately, we could work out an agreement. Along with his staff, we worked on legislation that combined education and prevention and left treatment issues to their individual offices. This was a major bill and after spending the night working on it, the governor brought it down to the MGM building in New York City for a press conference. He put his arm around my shoulder to congratulate me on the drafting of the creative ideas needed to pass the bill. A lesson learned from this experience is that you might be the opposition one day, but the next day be a close ally of your opponent if you can find the power to gain respect for the opinions of your constituency.

Officially a Disease – Dealing with the Alcoholic

Finally, legislation was passed that affirmed addiction as a disease. I believed in the virtues of the fellowship of Alcoholics Anonymous in treating the alcoholic. The insurance industry began to reimburse the treatment of alcoholism on par with the treatment of other illnesses, which led to a dramatic expansion in private and hospital-based inpatient treatment programs. In New York State, I felt like I was the goose that laid the golden egg for the insurance lobbying groups and insurance companies.

This brought about many difficult days of investigation and arguments under several administrations of state government. I tried to find systemic answers to the questions being raised by the problems I was encountering. I had come across people in our South End community who motivated me to go to the Capitol day after day because of their many personal tragedies.

Many significant problems, including an increase in crime, accompanied the opening of a methadone center next to the parish. We also worried that methadone was being given to children in our parish programs. These kids were rewarded for acting as watchdogs or mules transferring drugs, allowing the dealers to avoid having drugs on their person if caught.

One tragic example stands out in my mind. One day a young boy brought me to the top floor of one of the many empty buildings in our neighborhood, only to discover his 13-year-old brother lying dead. The boy's brother died holding an empty methadone container from the local health center in his hands. I called the police who brought the body to Albany Medical Center.

I kept asking the hospital to give the autopsy results to the boy's parents in an attempt to point out that methadone was the problem.

But this brought spokespersons for the medical and pharmaceutical companies and other advocates out of the woodwork. They fought my attempt to blame methadone for the death of this 13-year-old. In the end, I was cast as a person without credentials who made false and misleading statements.

Looking back upon my 50 years of experience with opioid abuse, I realize that its prevalence exploded when medical practitioners began prescribing opioids as painkillers. This has resulted in the fastest-growing cause of narcotics-related deaths. Much of this demand came about as doctors were encouraged by insurance companies to prescribe inexpensive painkillers. Advocacy for increased use led to methadone being dispensed by vending machines in California.

Many people are using OxyContin, Vicodin or Xanax, starting with a small dose prescribed by doctors without proper surveillance. The current trend is heroin and Fentanyl. Hospitals are using NARCAN to help save people who overdose, but they need to address this crisis with prevention and education, with supportive persons, places and things that will give users the hope of a continued recovery.

Following the identification of alcoholism as a disease, the healthcare system was not prepared to handle the drunks and their difficult lifestyles. Some of the criminal justice folks were happy to see that they could be off-loaded to someone else's turf. Others found that drunks were great in jail for their "trustee" status, a label given to more cooperative inmates. They cut grass, cooked food and cleaned the offices and administration rooms. Prison administrators regretted losing them and having to hire new, outside help.

I often heard about jails putting out the word that they needed a cook, and the cops would be dispatched to pick up one of their "favorites." Sometimes the person wasn't even drinking, but was picked up nonetheless and brought back to the facility and immediately assigned to the kitchen. These prisoners never really complained, because they knew that the warden appreciated their cooperation and there were rewards and special privileges to be had. Many wanted to go back to jail for a spell during the cold months because they'd be given soft jobs and a warm bed.

Another issue I had to deal with involved court cases Adjourned in Contemplation of Dismissal. The accused person had to admit his or her guilt; they were then assigned to a corrective program. I proposed a simple law that would allow such persons to be transported to the Catskill Mountains to help pick fruits and vegetables. But before they got on the bus, they were arrested for appearance in public under the influence and placed in the prison system. They did the work for minimum pay and lived in housing provided by the system. When they finished the job, their pay was taken from them to cover the cost of room and board.

This daily ritual of judges allowing men to choose our shelters over jail evolved into a formal program named Honor Court. It was established in 1983 with the help of Congressman Mike McNulty, Assemblyman Dick Conners and Senator Howard Nolan. It remains my most favorite program. Victor Brown, Sondra Koss and Sister Phyllis Herbert were the co-founders. Honor Court staff work closely with the district attorney, public defenders and other lawyers to divert offenders before they reach the court system. Many go on to work in our programs. I believe that once an addict becomes sober and abstinent, they want to give back. You cannot find much more talented people.

One of my most gratifying opportunities came from the Alcohol and Substance Abuse Training (ASAT) programs that I started in 1976 within the state Department of Correctional Services. The highlight was being able to set aside special recovery program dorms for veterans.

With more than 40,000 inmates in our ASAT programs, we were able to extend it to serve veterans. As a prison chaplain, I was eager to see the number of inmates who were quick to join. The veterans were most appreciative and did great work toward their recovery. Our local Assemblyman Dick Conners was always helpful in supporting positive aftercare that dramatically helped with a recovery lifestyle.

PART VI
A New Ministry

Albany to Bolton Landing

The thought of leaving St. John's Parish in the South End of Albany after 27 years (1959-1976) was deeply emotional for me. I was very happy there. I was beginning to think that I was at the peak of my ministry, able to contribute and having earned the support and respect to make things better in the lives of so many. I wanted to stay to see the miracles happen. I was discouraged about leaving and not looking forward to moving on to another assignment.

Two situations in my life ultimately made me realize I needed to move: One was a physical problem that required surgery on my knees, and the other a financial obligation for which I needed to make money to repay a long-standing debt of $200,000. The debt occurred when our truck driving school went into bankruptcy after ten years of operation.

Eventually, given my knee problems, which now required me to use a wheelchair and cane to get around, I decided to speak with the bishop. I told him I just needed to regain my health and mobility. He told me he just happened to have an assignment that would allow me to pastor a parish and eventually continue my ministry to people in the criminal justice system. He assigned me to Blessed Sacrament Parish in Bolton Landing, New York.

I arrived at Blessed Sacrament Parish in October of 1976. Fortunately, the rush of summer activities and crowds at Lake George and Bolton were slowing down, giving me time to adjust. When I left St. John's, I asked whether any of the men I knew in recovery wanted to join me in the North Country. I was blessed with George, who volunteered and arrived at the Parish two weeks after me.

George lived with me at the rectory and took care of routine tasks at the house: phone calls, answering the door, welcoming visitors and general administrative duties. He was also a great cook, a gift that I fully appreciated. The parishioners welcomed George. His support and loyalty mirrored what I received from the parish. He stayed with us for many years and when he died suddenly; his brother Joe came to take over his duties.

My first priority was to develop a vital parish council that would take on leadership roles in the various ministries of liturgy, faith formation, pastoral care, administration and coordination of social events. The leadership from the council and parish deacon was extraordinary. They were a model for how well parishioners and clergy could work together. They eventually allowed me to continue as chaplain at the Wilton prison and provide leadership in the field of alcoholism.

Too soon, I experienced my first summer as pastor in Bolton Landing. The pace of parish activity took on new life. We doubled masses, confessions, weddings and pastoral care services to accommodate the swell of summer visitors and residents.

Despite my initial apprehensions, it didn't take long for Bolton to become one of the most beautiful and incredible experiences of my life. As the saying goes, "addiction does not discriminate; it doesn't care if you are rich or poor." Before long, I found myself working with residents who needed treatment for addiction. I found the people here ready, willing and able to appreciate and understand the work I was doing.

These special families became and remain a mainstay in my support system. They became partners in serving the poor, especially those addicted to drugs and alcohol. They worked tirelessly to advance our PYHIT fundraising efforts, selling cookbooks, hosting holiday craft fairs and organizing Lake George cruises on the Mohican tour boat.

One parishioner, John Consaga, would frequently invite me to dinner at his amazing mountaintop home. He later joined our PYHIT Board of Directors and to this day is completely dedicated to our mission. Like John, many people in Bolton Landing became lifelong friends who I will never forget. I celebrated my twenty-fifth anniversary as a priest and my seventy-fifth birthday with them.

One story and liturgical event among so many stands out for me to this day: the celebration of the North American Martyrs and Blessed Kateri Tekakwitha in late August. The sanctuary was decorated to look woodsy and rustic, graced with evergreens, stuffed forest animals, birch tree branches and logs. The altar itself was an old canoe turned upside down, upon which the altar vessels, candles and books were placed. The children, dressed in costume, told the story of the martyrs and Blessed Kateri. I described how the original antique birch canoe was borrowed from Fort Ticonderoga, something we did each year to celebrate the event.

Later, at a dinner party held at the fort, the director invited me to give the invocation. Afterward, he announced to everyone that since I borrowed the canoe each year and was now retiring, he was gifting me the canoe to take with me. When the time came, I tied the canoe to the top of my car and drove down the Northway at about 35 miles per hour to the Mother Teresa Community in the South

End of Albany where I was scheduled to say mass. I later arranged to give the canoe to the Shrine of the North American Martyrs in Auriesville, New York.

I spent 30 years with the parish and people of Bolton Landing. It was with great regret that I had to leave the parish when I reached the mandatory retirement age of 75. After my retirement, I was invited back to Bolton Landing on many occasions. The Brady family invited me to stay at their magnificent home at Rocky Point on the lake. They placed an Adirondack chair beneath a shady tree where I would sit in the morning with my prayer book. The peace, beauty and solitude of that place made me so happy and relaxed.

A group of Blessed Sacrament parishioners even came to celebrate my ninetieth birthday on August 4, 2020. The door that God opened to Bolton Landing provided me with a faith-filled and joyous road on my journey.

Climbing Mount McGregor

I regained my mobility during my time in Bolton Landing, enabling me to visit local state prisons. When I got off crutches, I applied for the prison chaplain position at Mount McGregor Correctional Facility. I applied as a volunteer until I could be formally assigned.

It was all very familiar, helping parolees and teaching inmates how to prepare for community reintegration. It took a few years of working as a volunteer before I received the assignment, but the position was a winner because it gave me a new ministry that I loved. Going into Mount McGregor every day at 6:30am was a joy.

I trained some of the security staff at the Mount McGregor facility on how to provide both security and treatment. The Alcohol and Substance Abuse Training (ASAT) program was based on respect and responsibility. The security staff was delighted to have the opportunity to help turn inmates into taxpayers. It was a win for our inmate clients, for the security guards and for government funding sources.

What a change it made in my ministry! I had worked as a county chaplain for 18 years, but now I was in the state system. I was on the front line in a correctional facility and could see things that needed to be done to keep these men from getting into more trouble once they were released.

With the help of prison officials and friends in the New York State Department of Correctional Services, we launched several programs that became models for other facilities and states. These programs were designed to help the men learn to fight their addictions and return to their communities as responsible citizens. I was used to working with former inmates, but now I had the chance to work with them before their release, with more time than the county jail system allowed.

It was one of the happiest periods of my life. Working for 33 years in the county and state corrections systems gave me the chance to implement my ideas on how to help the addicted during their time of incarceration. I was doing what I loved, and they gave me a salary to do it!

I began to think about how to organize a program that would reward people who made a commitment to their recovery treatment while still in prison. I needed to give inmates an incentive to volunteer for the program.

First I approached the state parole board, asking them to accept my credentials so that my recommendations would carry some weight in the board's deliberations about an inmate's release. This was the reward I could offer participants who were successful in their ASAT program treatment. Once this was established, inmates quickly volunteered to join and comply with the program's rules and recommendations.

As director of the New York State Department of Corrections Alcohol and Substance Abuse Treatment programs, I would carefully explain the benefits of getting a positive parole letter to inmates. A letter recognized for merit time would help them gain an earlier release. Aware of that information, inmates were quick to participate and we avoided the need to mandate treatment for them. In too many cases, more negative inmates tried to persuade others that the treatment was unnecessary, adding that they would miss out on recreation time by signing up. An orientation about the benefits of cooperation as soon as inmates entered the facility helped defeat this negativity.

The truth is judges now include treatment recommendations in their presentencing reports. But based on my 33 years of experience working behind bars, I know that merely getting the inmates into the program is not sufficient; there needs to be a desire to participate and succeed. It is what we know as the third tradition in AA: "The only requirement for membership is a desire to stop drinking."

The word in the general prison population was that there were definite benefits to joining alcohol and substance abuse programs. If inmates feel their peers are okay with it, that opens the door. They join as willing volunteers. This is the key to a successful program, and the best way to promote a positive atmosphere is by using inmates as program staff in positions such as group leaders, clerks and video operators. This has always been an important tenet in therapeutic communities. It was also thought to be in conflict with the thinking behind American Correctional Association directives.

Our procedures needed to specify that civilian staff members always supervise the inmates. All paperwork required authorization by the civilians responsible for an inmate's daily duties. We encouraged the inmates to accept leadership roles and to be proud, but we did not allow them to have direct authority over other inmates. We had to ensure that their assignments would not violate correctional guidelines.

Assigning duties to inmates motivates them to buy into becoming "part of the solution" and challenges them to take pride in accepting the responsibilities of making the program work. They feel a sense of ownership because of their role as group leaders or program clerks. These leaders have become outstanding examples of successful recovery and are now working in the addiction field and within prison facilities. They are called "wounded healers" because of their dedication to the inmates and parolees. They can identify with the inmates and credibly claim to understand their needs. Bringing wounded healers back to work in prison programs is a valuable tool that encourages recovery and discourages recidivism.

We set up special dorms and day programming for inmates who agreed to participate in ASAT. The "carrot" worked. It wasn't long before we had a full house. We would break participants into groups of six who would work with an individual counselor. There were also large-group sessions held in the chapel for those who were just looking for general information. They would learn about the process of addiction, the process of recovery, the process of relapse prevention and understanding themselves or others.

The program consisted of six intensive months of treatment. The inmates began to buy into it and take ownership, realizing it would be of tremendous help once they were released to the outside community. Many inmates became wounded healers who continued in the field after their release. At Mount McGregor, we had more than 800 inmates participating in the ASAT programs. In the first years, our wounded healers were the only staff, but eventually, with the help of our legislative friends, we were able to obtain funding and hire some professional staff.

Esprit de corps grew among the addicted inmates. They were doing something about the problem that had landed most of them in prison, and they were doing it themselves. The corrections officers saw inmate behavior improve, so whenever we needed support from their union they were quick to assist. It is the self-help aspect of ASAT that made it so successful; the inmates volunteered to be helped by other inmates and professional staff.

We tried to make ASAT an "inmate-owned program." This was tricky because of American Correctional Association guidelines that state inmates cannot be placed in positions of power over other inmates. Therefore, our ASAT staff supervised everyone. In reality, our civilian staff was in control, but they left many details of day-to-day operations in the hands of carefully selected and trained inmates. Our staff helped them get placed in positive aftercare experiences as a reward for their dedicated involvement with their dorm or cellblock.

While we concentrated on the inmates, we also needed to think about the security staff and bring them in as part of the team. The inmates were taught to respect the security staff and vice-versa. Introducing a treatment mentality created a more relaxed environment for all involved and a win-win for the program. Cooperation between the inmates and security staff reduced costs for overtime, double coverage, rover coverage and SWAT teams.

The success of our Mount McGregor Correctional Facility Alcohol and Substance Abuse Training program did not go unnoticed. The administration appreciated the savings and encouraged other superintendents to bring ASAT into their facilities. The fiscal savings resulted in other administrative leaders agreeing to expansion opportunities.

The union opposed our programs at first. But once they recognized that ASAT resulted in a more relaxed and enjoyable work environment, union leadership advocated with us for expansion and additional funding. It was all part of the win-win experience that made it successful.

Transitioning to a campus-like setting at prisons was a new experiment for the Department of Correctional Services, but one it came to appreciate—especially the older officers who were getting close to retirement. They had seniority in bidding on preferred jobs within a prison and would usually select our dorms. It was the cooperative efforts of civilians and inmates that kept dorms free of problems and focused on treatment issues.

The idea was to keep inmates busy and treatment-centered without the problems that traditionally happen within a prison population. When I talk about a "win-win," I'm including all of the prison staff, administration and inmates. A study by the criminal justice graduate school at SUNY showed that inmates in the Mount McGregor ASAT program had less than a 10% re-incarceration rate over a 10-year period. This applied to ASAT inmates with access to drug-free housing, treatment and a job after being released.

We found that when we were unable to support inmates with these resources, their re-incarceration rate increased by about 20%. That's why our focus for the past 50 years has been to find clients affordable housing, keep them in treatment and get them a job with a decent career path.

Housing opportunities in New York City, where the majority of inmates once lived, were difficult to find due to the high cost of buying or renting properties. In some distressed parts of upstate New

York, we were able to achieve the preferred one-third of income goes to housing formula. This gives the individual the time to maintain his or her recovery in an affordable, drug-free setting.

The jobs we provided guaranteed clients work experience because our agency owned several of the industries. We could quickly place someone with a difficult felony record in our job internship program and help them build at least a six-month resume of success and then encourage them to seek better opportunities in the larger job market. We sought out agreements with employers who found our vocational placements to be above average compared to mainstream job placement agencies. This reputation opened the door to upgrading our clients to permanent jobs in the private sector.

Mount McGregor was a great opportunity to link inmates into a group. I taught them about the disease of addiction based on my experience at St. John's and from what I had learned over the years from experts in the field. The inmate I chose for our first program proved to be the right selection, someone who challenged all others to follow his example. After interviewing several candidates for the position, I was approached by an inmate who had been in prison for 27 years. He weighed more than 300 pounds, earning him the nickname "the monster." True to his name, he implemented what was called the "Monster Concept" of using therapy ideas.

I also taught daily groups using the strong philosophy of the 12-step fellowship model. I would spend most of my time trying to set up "disease concept" classes that would become part of the everyday schedule. Having written the law that decriminalized public intoxication in New York State—legislation that would soon become the model for many other states—you can imagine the joy of having the chance to prove that a program of recovery would win out over incarceration.

Alcohol and Substance Abuse Training (ASAT) Rules

Getting participants to become part of a team creates a spirit of cooperation that gives them the courage to break the "inmate code." Inmate leaders willing to break the code are special people. Our selected leader took on a powerful, well-connected crime network inside the prison. He confronted another inmate operating a drug delivery system for violating our clean-and-sober ASAT dorm rules. Our coordinator told the offender to walk to the toilet and flush his score down the drain, allowing that he could return once he decided to abide by the rules of the program.

The four ASAT rules were very simple: no illicit sex, no stealing, no threats of physical harm and no drug use. All of the other violations were called "pull ups," meaning the inmate staff and civilian counselor would bring the inmate into a quiet room to see if he was receptive to their advice. If that didn't work, we would call a general meeting of the dorm members and the group would confront the person who was being uncooperative. Usually, the person acquiesced immediately and was given another chance to stay with the program.

Word got out to the population that the program was sincere and that nobody would be able to get a certificate without positive ASAT participation. When security saw the sincerity of the program, the corrections officers and administration bought into it. Soon, they were quick to testify at legislative hearings to maintain it. The savings for New York State were enormous because of the lack of confrontations, tier hearings and security overtime. It was a "win-win" for the officers, the inmates and the state. Some jobs were lost, but the officers were happy with the relaxed workload and more peaceful atmosphere, which promoted the "correctional" aspect of the facility. We instituted a day-in treatment program at Mount McGregor and in stages created a residential dorm that improved the quality of life until the inmates were released.

These programs were extremely successful. They produced many wounded healers who still work in the field of addiction, both outside and inside correctional facilities. These men became so dedicated to the idea of recovery that they were willing to return to the places where they were once incarcerated to spread the news of recovery and hope of a better way of life.

This was a whole new chapter in my multifaceted ministry. Through our system of treatment, clean and sober housing and job training, we helped people turn away from crime and become taxpaying citizens once again. It worked! The recidivism rate in 1998 was less than 10%. Participants had a plan after prison for drug-free living with treatment and training that led to a job. They were no longer "all dressed up with no place to go!"

My life turned on the programs for re-entry and community reintegration. It became much easier to go to legislators and their staffs, because we had the numbers to prove we could do this more efficiently and save the taxpayers money. When I retired in 1990, there were 41,000 inmates in ASAT programs all across New York State. That all grew out of the first program I founded at Mount McGregor in 1976.

Proven Success

In all of my 50-plus years of working with inmates and parolees, a basic principle of giving and getting respect has persisted. It is foundational to the success of all our programs, in and out of prisons. It sets the standard for what a client can expect as the reward in a preferred aftercare plan, one that offers a parolee a supportive network of treatment, safe, affordable housing, and the promise of a job upon completion of the necessary training.

When you promise a parolee successful community reintegration, your word becomes a bonded agreement. You have to give them a specific set of conditions for participation that puts the weight on their cooperation in exchange for the promised support. This is what produces a win 90% of the time, and letting them know it's possible to be a winner is important. When we have clients reaching out for help, we must be sure they understand that failure will result in privileges being withheld—making sure they know that their lack of cooperation was the cause.

My philosophy has always been to take away any excuses. Too often, a parolee will present a well-planned list of excuses when parole is violated—an attempt to solicit sympathy and keep their freedom. My goal is to show that they must surrender to the better ways of a life in recovery. They must be accountable for their actions. When you remove the excuses, it sends a positive message to others watching.

Our goal of turning parolees into taxpayers is the mission statement of all our programs. Parolees need to understand where they are going and how to get there. That is why we call it the "Glidepath to Recovery."

I visualized the "glidepath" idea while watching the film Midway, where pilots on an aircraft carrier guided their planes to safe landings.

Like pilots doing what they've been trained to do, people who are sincere about their recovery are waved in, while those who are lack commitment are waved off and must try again. We never hesitated to re-admit inmates once they committed to treatment of their disease. I've always said, "Our car goes forward, and also in reverse."

Not all clients are admitted to our aftercare programs. We weed out those who are just "fronting the sober" with no real commitment. People who make it clear they are not going to cooperate and make life miserable for others who want to be in the program are waved aside.

The ASAT program spread from Mount McGregor to other correctional facilities in the system. When I retired from corrections, the program existed in 57 of the 70 state facilities in one form or another. It has worked successfully since 1976. We tried to build a program in the Department of Correctional Services that would prove to be less expensive, and it happened. We challenged inmates to carry the message of recovery that could be emulated by others.

My dream in running the ASAT program for 40,000 inmates was to expand aftercare in the community and pave the way for a road to recovery. I had to rev up to expand my footprint and went all over the state to find facilities that would meet local zoning and planning requirements. Our ASAT graduates, solid role models like Clarence Carter and Lloyd Middleton, managed the programs.

We provided vocational training through the state Education Department's Office of Vocational Rehabilitation. At the same time, our clients received housing and treatment in a seamless manner. We placed graduates in the Local 471 Hotel and Restaurant Employees Union to improve their opportunities for a better future.

This was all happening in the late 1970s and early 1980s and now, 50 years later, the field has bought into the concept. At that time, the treatment philosophy was to keep someone in treatment for over a year. The emphasis was not on employment. Not only have I been in the right place at the right time, I've also been ahead of my time.

Shadd Maruna, professor of criminology at the SUNY School of Criminal Justice, became interested in the success of our program. He spent a lot of time studying ASAT and our community aftercare models. In his study, Shadd concluded that ASAT graduates who completed our aftercare program in the community had a recidivism rate that was less than 12%, compared to 32% for those who were released without a program in the community. He talks about the program in his book, *Making Good: How Ex-Convicts Reform and Rebuild Their Lives*, which was named the Outstanding Contribution to Criminology by the American Society of Criminology In 2001. Shadd has also received awards from the Howard League for Penal Reform and the Economic and Social Research for his work's impact on penal policy.

Community-Based Residential Programs

In the 1990s, the New York City Human Resource Agency funded housing for our ASAT graduates at Altamont House in Altamont, NY, and the Schuyler Inn in Menands, NY. It was a great success because when you take a person away from certain people, places and things, they become productive citizens supporting themselves and their communities.

Community block grant funding took precedent over programs and all inmates had to be paroled to their county of commitment. Thus, my quest to find aftercare in every major city began. In 1995, the state Sentencing Reform Act created a major new diversion program, the Willard Drug Treatment Campus. Its purpose was to divert second felony offenders with substance abuse problems from commitment to the Department of Corrections. This resulted in a shrinking ASAT pool. However, we enjoyed a great relationship with the Division of Parole. Friends like Jim Torriani, John Lowery, Pat Fitzmaurice, Ed Frailey and Janet Reeves truly cared about the clients and we entered into a contract for parole stabilization beds and later the community-based residential program. In these programs, the inmate was transferred directly from the correctional facility to one of our beds because of the groundwork we had done. We had beds in Queens, Albany, Syracuse and Buffalo. We were able to shift our focus from ASAT to the Parole Division.

The Dignity of a Paycheck

When I arrived in 1959, I found out that most men in our South End community needed employment. It became my new priority and I immediately recognized my mission: create paying jobs to help the disenfranchised become taxpayers.

Challenged to defeat negative perceptions about our friends arriving from the south, our social ministry's strategy was to get them the dignity of a job by helping with their preparation and connecting them with our Albany friends. Many women from the south came with children and New York State laws required that the father support them. But where could they find a job? Most opportunities were closed to them and they would then face arrest for not paying child support. It was a no-win situation for keeping families together resulting in a matriarchal society. Our efforts focused on finding men jobs to preserve family unity and the fathers' pride.

As a Catholic priest in Albany, local leaders listened to what our folks needed. I would set up meetings with industry bosses that would introduce new ideas and open doors to potential program opportunities.

For years, I teamed up with Larry Burwell, Sam McDowell, Elder Jack Johnson, Lew Swyer and leaders of the Urban League to provide new arrivals from the south with a job. Our school parents at St. John's had problems getting any type of employment. I would spend much of my free time searching for job opportunities for them. The "Brothers," a great group of young Black men including Leon Van Dyke and Buster Parker, helped the Black community in their quest for employment.

It was extremely difficult for minorities to find a job in the 1950s. Opportunities were limited because of the barriers that existed. A minority could find service jobs, but not in any office, tech or professional position.

My ideas centered on what was possible in the inner city. Many job opportunities were moving to the suburbs—a major problem for men without cars. So, I started a cleaning company, a landscaping business and a placement agency. When the Selkirk Rail Yard opened just south of Albany, I formed a tractor-trailer driving school.

I purchased big-rig tractor-trailer trucks and supported the training of about 20 drivers in 12-week classes, all with limited funds. The drivers were placed in new positions created by the 1964 Johnson Great Society Act.

As a partner with E. Phillip Randolph, I had access to the Capitol and heard about the Highway Act of 1956, which led to the development of 41,000 miles of interstate highways. In the 1960s, I saw the expansion that was happening in the Port of Albany and Selkirk Rail Yard as an opportunity. I quickly thought about the law: When you cross state lines, you must include minority drivers in your fleet. The law stated, "To drive interstate, equal opportunities were required."

My idea was twofold: train Black drivers and then open the

program up to parents in our school so the men would have money to pay the tuition. We had a Parent-Teacher Association at our school of 280 students, most of whom were Black. Only one father was listed as a PTA member.

The fathers continued to face fewer job opportunities, lower pay, poorer benefits and greater job instability. They were absent in family life to allow the women to receive financial assistance. If paternity could be established, the father was issued a warrant for nonpayment of child support.

Working with Bill Murray, who knew all of the rules and regulations of the state Education Department as a former employee, we rented space in East Greenbush, New York. Once established, the school averaged 24 men per class. This gave me reason to contact my friends in trucking companies who verified that they needed as many qualified minority drivers as possible. It was a win for our most needy men and for the Department of Transportation, which received very dedicated drivers.

The Teamsters Union eventually came after me, claiming I was not the right person to train people. I told them New York State had proven our drivers to be qualified and our course was certified by the state Education Department.

Then the trouble started with damage to our equipment: sugar in the gas tanks, transmissions destroyed and other mandated safety equipment compromised.

The Dunn Memorial Bridge was demolished using dynamite in 1971 to make way for its replacement, a span that would connect the Empire State Plaza with the highway. I was never sure whether it was the teamsters or the dynamite that caused $8,300 worth of broken windows in our school. The driving school became a never-ending battle, but all of our graduates got jobs. It only ended because we could no longer afford the damages.

Eventually, the teamsters no longer viewed me as an enemy and I enjoyed a great relationship with Whitey Bennett and John Bulgaro. We worked together to find employment opportunities for our clients. The teamsters enrolled them in their Commercial Drivers License school and then helped them find jobs.

The men's paychecks circulated within our South End community supporting the many small local businesses. The big-box stores that now dominate the retail economy offer no such benefits to the many community businesses in need. Jobs became my priority, and I am still an advocate for employment with our mission to "create taxpayers." History has proven that "ghetto" jobs are necessary so local residents can motivate each other as example of success. "Each one, teach one."

The frustrations of the 1960s were valuable learning tools in figuring out how to get people jobs. The dignity of a paycheck has always been a priority. I've always believed that employment is key to improving the lives of the addicted. For people in recovery, it has both economic and non-economic benefits. Work provides structure, an opportunity for social connections and socialization with others who can serve as role models. It makes a person feel valued and respected in the community. It is especially important for those who have been stigmatized and discriminated against. More importantly, employment can strengthen a person's commitment to recovery.

While trying to get legislators to accept the idea of decriminalization, our program operated a former Holiday Inn that became the home for our culinary and hospitality training school. We renamed the facility the Schuyler Inn. It was a great program that created much-needed job opportunities. I had hundreds of clients who needed employment and the hotel and hospitality union needed trained, qualified workers. This became a great partnership that gave our clients the dignity of a paycheck.

Our mission was to create taxpayers and now we were under contract as the hospitality union's official training partner. The greatest bonus came when their president said I would need to interview someone from the union staff to lead our program. It turned out to be a transformational moment when Jackie Gentile joined our agency. With her amazing talents, she was the person guiding all of our growth with her innovative ideas. She created synergy and provided supervision as our chief of operations.

Jackie watched over our statewide treatment, housing, education and employment programs. She had the flexible thinking needed to coordinate all of the programs and personalities. We stressed the motto, "Blessed are the flexible for they are less likely to get bent out of shape." Jackie modeled this philosophy, which was so essential to our PYHIT agency teamwork.

Our Schuyler Inn included a fully operational hotel and banquet center. We secured a contract to house visiting college students while operating the hotel, which provided us with some interesting experiences. When a group of Russian female students stayed with us on a warm summer day, I received a call from our front desk telling me that there was a large crowd gathering at our pool because the guests were all swimming in the nude. Local village leaders encouraged us to fill in the pool and we quickly agreed.

We also hosted a Uganda national dance and music tour group of 40 who were stranded in Albany. Their sponsor took all of their money and their airline tickets leaving them without any way to get home. They were sent to our hotel and we were asked to assist them. They stayed with us for four months and we arranged for them to visit any schools and institutions that would pay them $300 for a performance. They were outstanding and we were getting them several shows a week. I made all of the calls and in the end, we had to raise over $100,000 to get them back home. Eventually we were able to bring them to JFK airport for their return home.

In appreciation of our hospitality, they named a school for us. We still hear from some of these joyful folks who were willing to entertain us and other audiences. Their stay enriched us all. They were respectful of our staff and created a wonderful relationship with the Capital District community.

We were also housing homeless veterans while operating our state-certified culinary school and our food services, which were open to the public. In addition, the hotel served many of our former clients from the Eleanor House in Selkirk, NY, a necessary step for our financial stability. Selkirk was a large 80-bedroom facility operated as a female domestic violence shelter. It was developed because so many women came forward with sad stories of being trapped by their addiction with no way to help their families.

We attempted to serve women coming from emergency situations. For instance, "street walkers" from Rochester, NY, contacted us for help in breaking the hold their pimps had over them. The women would be rewarded with drugs as long as they continued to bring in prostitution money. I would get the call saying, "Can you meet our friend getting off at the bus station tonight at 11?" I would be there to welcome them and bring them to our Selkirk program. It was a significant savings for the agencies that sent them, but a large cost to us.

The majority of the women at Selkirk were released to our community reintegration program, which allowed them to get their children back from child protective services. Because of state block grant funding rules, our local leaders refused to accept any financial responsibility for these "outsiders." The total allotment for a family of four at that time was an average of $320 a month. Compare that to the cost of housing a mother in jail and her children in county protective custody care. It's less than one-tenth, and yet counties refused to cooperate with other sites and to work out payment agreements.

In our original video describing the "Glidepath to Recovery," I had my arms around two boys and their mom, who was doing well in our Selkirk recovery program. Two months later, her mother called me to say that her daughter had gone back on the street and was found in a dumpster at a motel in the west end of Albany. She was a wonderful woman and her mother and I still have nightmares about this sad story. It just didn't have to happen!

Our success with addicted women was amazing. Over 80% achieved sobriety and with vocational training were able to support their family. The bank that financed our Selkirk program soon recognized our losses and we were forced to close the program to save our other mortgages. In order to continue serving this homeless female population, we purchased apartment houses in Albany, which also lost money. Later, most homeless women were sheltered at the Schuyler Inn with the help of local counties that covered the cost of our services.

Friends Along the Way

Reflecting on my relocation from St. John's Parish in inner city Albany to Blessed Sacrament in Bolton Landing, which led to my involvement with the state prison system, I realize the changes that ASAT made in the inmates' lives was a great gift. We helped put thousands of inmates on a successful path to a better, sober, clean life.

For many years, I've depended on inmates who came into our program and accepted a leadership role. One of the most outstanding of them was Tyler Trice. He was a sought-after basketball player in New York City, but instead of getting a scholarship and completing college, he got into drugs. As a result, he lost about 20 years of his life to a battle with addiction and incarceration. Tyler spent his remaining days assisting others with the same problems. He founded our Albany Recovery Tenants Association, ran for school board and was invited to sit on the boards of many recovery agencies. Tyler became a winner in all respects. I thought about his experiences when I delivered the eulogy at his funeral. Seeing men and women like Tyler return to become contributing members of society are among the most rewarding accomplishments of my life.

I also think about the legislators who have supported my efforts to change laws in favor of the addicted and homeless. I'm thankful for the countless persons I had the privilege to call close friends. Aside from those I've already mentioned, there were Senators Jack Bronston and George Mitchell. In 1959, their legislation enabled us to begin a study to evaluate how alcoholics would be best served in a setting other than in jail. Senator William Roth wrote legislation that positively impacted people who were incarcerated. Senator Lee Metcalf addressed public health laws. My own senator from Albany was Julian Erway, but as a Democrat he did not have much power in a GOP-controlled senate. Senators Kirk Watson and George Mitchell sponsored a $200,000 budget bill to fund start-up treatment programs for the addicted.

In the Assembly, encouragement came from leaders Max Turshen, Julius Volker and Peter Lawrence. Senator John Hughes of Syracuse put money into the counties with the hope it would encourage local support to start alcoholism treatment programs. Funds were also provided by Assemblyman Julius Volker to start councils on alcoholism. Later, his son Senator Dale Volker provided the resources for local advocates around the state to establish programs at the county level. Senator Metcalf, a former housing director from Auburn, New York, became a strong advocate for health programs, as did Senator Bill Conklin, who championed anyone with a disability.

Some great senators came to Albany in 1960. I would go out to dinner at least twice a week with Senator Tom Laverne of Rochester. I enjoyed joking with Senator Edward Lentol, who came to the Senate after serving as sewer commissioner in Brooklyn.

It was during this period that the rules committee passed an outpatient program bill that gave our constituency a very positive Medicaid reimbursement, accompanied by an explosion of services around the state.

Although heroin use has reached epidemic levels in a short time, it is not new to our culture. When assigned as a newly ordained priest to St. John's, I began with the question: "What are the needs in the parish and in the South End of Albany"? Addiction and homelessness were of major concern. For years, the parish community of St. John's was engaged in social issues and outreach to the larger South End population. Heroin was the predominant drug and clients with a sincere desire to stop using were given an opportunity for recovery.

Unfortunately, media reports during my 18 years at the parish were more focused on negative police court stories and less on the positive impact of our open-door policy and support from the parish and community. The media wasn't receptive to reporting on merciful deeds.

The work of Pope Francis and his challenging for the works of mercy with our open door to these needs and the beatitudes will keep us focused with Jesus.

On January 1, 2015, my friend Mario died. I had a great relationship with Governor Mario Cuomo and it was fun whenever we had time to talk. We swapped baseball stories and I would play basketball with him at night.

I would meet him on the dais as chaplain of the state Senate when he was governor. If a vote was delayed, he would lean over to me and say, "Pick out someone." I would name a controversial person from the Middle Ages. We would begin a private, often emotional debate and the members would ask, "What are they arguing about?"

Mario would call me late at night to talk about a game I had officiated for our Capitol basketball league. I started the league with Assembly Deputy Speaker Bill Passannante. Mario played and he was always very competitive, challenging my calls on fouls and other violations. I got used to the debates and emotions that went with them. The next day, it was never a problem and we would laugh about our differences.

The political wisdom of our agency board chairman Bill Hennessey was a blessing. He served as state commissioner of transportation, chair of the New York State Thruway Authority and chair of the state Democratic Party. Before Mario was ever thought of as a possible nominee for governor, Mayor Corning and Bill Hennessey proposed his name and helped him organize his campaign.

Bill and I would discuss ideas for our agency just about every Saturday morning; Mario would invariably call to suggest nominees for the authority. Bill frequently disagreed and the call would become a hot one. Bill warned Mario that I was with him and would be caught up in the discussion. He never hesitated to speak his mind, even if Mario didn't to want to hear it. They admired each other and didn't need written agreements. Both believed a handshake was sufficient.

What I enjoyed most about Mario was his commitment and desire for honest feedback. I never feared any kind of retaliation would result from our many differing opinions.

My mom was frequently at meetings and when Mario spotted her he would ask her to stand and thank her for my work on behalf of the needy. She told me how much she loved him and how proud she felt afterward.

NIMBY

My friend David Paterson had a difficult year in 2008 after taking over as governor following the Eliot Spitzer prostitution scandal. I always had a great relationship with Governor Patterson. When he was a humble senator, we would go out at night for pizza or some other kind of meal. He was a person who respected everyone on both sides of the political aisle.

This brings to mind a problem that I feel existed in the Capitol early on and continues today. There are few hero-type leaders we can look at and ask our students to admire. Having been around the Capitol for 50 years, I'm very aware of the scandals and the constant need to raise money for the next election. It all brings little joy to constituents, who are always seeking support for their many needs, and frequently turn to attending a chicken dinner fundraiser.

Among those who helped with our re-entry issues—reintegrating clients into the community—was Ray Joyce. We owe a lot to this amazing person for his past leadership as a PYHIT board member. As chairman of the Albany Planning and Zoning Committee for over 30 years, Ray had the respect of community leaders not only in Albany but throughout the state as well.

Ray and I frequently discussed the issues of "NIMBY" (not in my backyard). I let him know that we needed help with many of our expansion efforts around the state. Other zoning and planning leaders from across New York often contacted Ray asking for information about our agency and the Albany experience. When considering a new site for re-entry services, we had to go to local officials to obtain approval for housing people returning from incarceration. With over 40,000 participants in ASAT looking for aftercare, we had to plan for their return to local catchment areas with supervision. Albany was the most resource-rich addiction recovery community in the U.S. Ray's support helped validate our "Glidepath to Recovery" model during a time of white flight from many inner cities in New York State.

There is always the fear that locals will reject our program in their community. My worst experience was in Poughkeepsie. We needed housing for six chefs from that area who were being placed in jobs. It sounds simple, but their parole supervisors asked us to get required code approvals from the community. A hearing was held with hundreds of locals in attendance. We told them about these men returning home with a year of recovery to their credit and with guaranteed jobs at local union hotels. The first person to stand up and speak said, "That's my son and I never want to see him again."

Having experienced more than a hundred of these types of meetings, people always want to know more about who you are and what happens in our program. They would speak with others like Ray and feel relaxed enough to grant their permission. Without his words of wisdom and knack for bonding, thousands of clients would have been returned to prison. Ray had the quiet courage to help inmates and prepare them for community reintegration.

PART VII
Retirement

Admit, Accept and Surrender

Admit, Accept and Surrender were three words that I used when talking to our clients, hoping they might help them in their recovery. As a guy in his mid-80s, my plans were to enjoy visiting our recovery programs in New York State to encourage our clients. I loved sharing the history of how inspired I was 50 years ago, meeting with Bill Wilson and many of the early leaders of the AA fellowship. Their wisdom continues to inspire me and I plan to continue to pass it forward. I might compare this to the friendly role of a grandfather sharing some of the history of those early days. Unfortunately, my dream of visiting clients to share inspirational stories had to be put on hold. An internal administrative situation consumed all of my attention. The problem was urgent and immediate since it questioned the integrity of our staff, programs and overall mission.

The program had been running well for many years. We had our ups and downs, of course. Then, in 2011, it was brought to my attention that we had an internal problem. We suspected that a staff member was stealing money from our six nonprofit corporations.

An internal investigation discovered the alleged wrongdoing. One of our longtime employees was accused of using program resources for personal gain. We decided to report the problem to our funding source, the state Office Alcohol and Substance Abuse Services (OASAS). They in turn reported it to the Commission on Quality of Care for review.

The problem resulted in the termination of the director of treatment programs. Our staff was divided on how to come together to restore confidence in PYHIT. It was a sad time and I felt betrayed by people I had trusted. Administrative staff tried to heal the division, but some resented the effort. In anger, a staff member who refused to work in our administrative office wrote a letter to our funding sources, to the attorney general and to the FBI, triggering a widespread investigation of our program.

We gave the Commission on Quality of Care full access to all of our programs and every piece of paperwork related to them. They set up shop in our Schenectady administrative building for over a year, even though their headquarters were just two miles away. We fully encouraged them to review our operations thoroughly and recommend improvements. We were the first OASAS agency that they ever scrutinized so closely.

The evidence we provided was then referred to the attorney general's office for its investigation. This led to our worst media day ever on December 12, 2012.

At 9am that day, the FBI raided the Schuyler Inn, our administrative office in Schenectady, and our Eagle Street office. The bureau brought in trucks and seized our computers and files from each of the locations. The first call came from Margie Reilly, director of development, saying that there was a mouse in her office. I called the exterminator who promised he would be there by 9am. The second call came from the Schuyler Inn asking, "Father, do you have a press conference here this morning?" We did not. Next, the Schenectady office called and said that FBI agents and police had come and locked the staff in a room.

I left immediately to find out what it was going on. I met with a friendly FBI agent who said, "We were all wondering who you are because we had to bring in staff and raid teams from all over the state to close down your operation." Later in the day he told me they could only get five agents for the John Gotti arrest, which made him wonder why they had brought in such a powerful force and given the media advance notice to ensure there would be film and photos.

It was the same kind of chaos at all of the sites. Margie, expecting the pest control staff, was quick to tell the FBI, "The mouse just ran under the printer!" Meanwhile agents had surrounded the building and closed off Eagle Street. Dressed in SWAT gear, they approached Margie, who was shocked by their number. Both Margie and the FBI were wondering what was going on.

Several months later, we continued to ask for our records back so we could complete internal audits and file required reports with state and federal funding sources.

When attempting to serve the addicted, the homeless and people in the criminal justice system, you become a prime target for the media. Several stories elevated in the press hampered our ability to raise money and provide services. One was about a young man who was staying at our Altamont property and requested permission to go to the hospital for the birth of his child. He had been arrested for possessing a small amount of marijuana and was sent to our treatment program under the jurisdiction of local authorities. We called to obtain their permission for him to go to Kingston Hospital. They agreed and when he came back to Altamont, I asked him how it went. He said that he was put in an ambulance and transported to Poughkeepsie because his wife required medical assistance. I told him that was not the permission that was agreed to, and I would have to report the incident to the authorities. They said, "Take away his television privileges for a short time and we'll drive out to have him sign the change order."

Soon, two officers arrived at the door and we called the new father down to explain what happened. The officers met him and suggested going to the kitchen to get a coffee. He was nervous and went to the bathroom. By the time the officers returned, he had taken off. Police cars from all over the area arrived and as did helicopters with their loudspeakers blaring that a criminal had escaped from Father Young's program. They set up roadblocks at Crossgate Mall and inspected all of the cars traveling on local highways.

Not only did they create a traffic jam at 5pm for many hours, they also went into area homes waving guns warning of an escaped convict. Police vehicles with loudspeakers continued to patrol the area warning the community of the danger.

Meanwhile, the "fugitive" they were looking for walked out of our building to meet them asking, "What's going on?"

Our van driver said, "They're looking for you."

"I never left the building," said the new dad.

Local code officials closed our building and I had to appear at their meetings and on television seven times to discuss how to correct the problem. I called the office supervising our client and they said, "All we wanted was to ask him to sign the no-television agreement for two more weeks, for our files."

Our losses were well over $1.5 million. Nothing happened to our client, but the authorities told me the police were happy to participate because it was a great training opportunity. It was in the headlines for days; our fundraising became the biggest loser. We're very grateful for the understanding of our Altamont and Guilderland leaders who have permitted our program and extended their hospitality for well over 30 years.

I mentioned our philosophy of admit, accept and surrender earlier. Well, I must now *admit* that some of our difficulties reported in the news stem from our efforts to keep the staff small and put more resources into the clients we're serving. It was a penny-wise and pound-foolish mistake.

That said, it's hard to apologize for generously taking care of people by giving them emergency money to improve their living conditions, or to pay those bills they couldn't handle while incarcerated. I've always been amazed at the amount of money I gave to people who needed to get back home in the south for a family funeral or related expenses.

Since that infamous date of December 12, 2012, we have expanded our administrative staff and hope to soon catch up with the very demanding paperwork required by all of our income sources. We used to enjoy some time to share fellowship memories with our counselors. Now they're always so busy meeting the reporting demands that it's all business. Lost is the feeling of genuine engagement with our clients.

Most of our staff are in their own recovery and want to share their experiences, strength and hope with their clients, but they just don't have the time because of the paperwork. I hear all of the time that it is not a happy experience being a counselor today.

Another mistake we made was relying on audits of our programs by leading accounting firms and funding sources. The way we paid our staff created a major problem, with our payroll listing them as either a consultant or as hourly staff. With over 500 employees and more than 100 program sites, it was a complicated payroll. Our Human Resources staff wanted a standard response to issue a paycheck, and they were quick to list all of our people as hourly employees. With our treatment staff that was not a problem, since they all worked in offices. But staff providing outreach in the field didn't keep office hours. It came down to the duties of a consultant versus those of an hourly employee, and we never broke down the difference in our reporting to the payroll service. The audits considered this a false accounting of their services.

When considering the accept and surrender philosophy, I must admit that when the state speaks—with all of its power—a small nonprofit like ours just doesn't have the resources to win even the most noble fight. On top of that, the state is always piling on unfunded mandates. We had no choice but to surrender to their demands in order to continue providing services to over 16,000 clients who depend on our help for their recovery, a paycheck and their dignity.

The attorney general's team interviewed some of our staff and asked them to persuade me to tell all I that know about New York State legislators. As their chaplain for 55 years, I was asked to help with many of their personal problems. They might be about who was a no-show, who has an alcohol or drug problem, or who has a girlfriend on the payroll? They told our COO Jackie that they would drop any charges against her if she could get me to give up evidence that would lead to as many convictions as possible. Meanwhile, the charges against Jackie amounted to issues with how paperwork was completed.

The kind of confidence that I have always kept is needed for a priest to be effective. Investigators said it would benefit my legacy to be known for assisting in the arrest of corrupt leaders. I'm trying to understand the position that now is being taken by our legal authorities.

During the investigation, reports coming from the depositions at my grand jury and those of our COO were difficult to hear. Investigators concocted fictitious stories to support their presumptions about what could have happened. Staff members who worked exclusively in our administration office in Schenectady had to admit they didn't know many of the 550 employees at our 117 program sites. This was used to support the allegation that many were no-show positions.

Paperwork was maintained at the various remote sites because of the trust and spirit of our dedicated staff; we enjoyed a team ministry. Unfortunately, we lost our mission of the beatitudes, which gave way to bureaucracy. Mistakes can become crimes with no criminal intent when serving clients using public money.

When we discovered the theft by one of our administrators, he wanted our agency to take all of his assets—his home, cars and all of his possessions—to compensate for what he had stolen. We didn't know the exact amount he had taken, but we turned him into the authorities. Afterward, we had to reduce our client services from 15,000 to less than 7,000 because of financial stress caused by legal and increased operational costs.

After seeing the evidence behind the charges that put our COO through the embarrassment of court appearances, I was totally distressed. I have known Jackie Gentile to be the most honest and dedicated person in our agency. Her work, her ministry, was a sense of mission, not a job.

When the judge questioned the assistant attorney general, he acknowledged that no money was missing under our administration's watch. We never received an official report from the attorney general and the matter has dragged on for years. It brings back the lessons of our background in Scripture that is lacking in those who created this trauma for our agency.

The offenders, the administrator mentioned earlier and a couple of others, are all examples of greed. Those who stole from our agency felt they were the only ones saying, "They worked hard and therefore deserved to take what they thought would be their deserved worth" without accountability. It was difficult to fathom because I know we had done so much for them. To me the lesson is in the parable of the Prodigal Son (Luke 15: 25-30) and the greed of these three staff members. But, in their case, we have not heard of any apology for their deeds.

Those who stole had me thinking of Matthew 20: 1-16 in the parable of the vineyard workers. They were jealous of those who were chosen and their envy became their "taking each other's inventory."

The case is also plainly stated in the *Big Book*. Resentment destroys more alcoholics than anything else does. A person stuck in resentment does not recover from addiction. Resentment can intoxicate a person, as feelings of anger and rage lead to a false sense of power.

The state blocked us from applying for any New York State contracts through the Grants Gateway program. This is a prequalification process not-for-profits use to apply for state funding. This ban has been difficult because it takes away hundreds of job opportunities for our clients who have been placed without the dignity of a paycheck.

In an attempt to maintain services for our clients, we have sold several buildings and terminated several hundred staff. We lost thousands of clients from our network of care who now live without access to the glide path to becoming a clean and sober taxpayer. For them, it closed the door of mercy.

Reflecting on Pope Francis' letter regarding mercy, I felt a personal connection to what he wrote: "Living on the outermost fringes of society" can be felt and verified when working with our clients. A challenge in this ministry is that hope be given to those needing it most.

Many times I was accused of being a friend of the criminals and addicts—even considered one of them because of my close friendships. It happened in 2011, when New York State investigations made them say I was one of the criminals. Now I've been blocked from helping those who call, write or visit daily asking me for help with the many difficulties of community reintegration.

When I met with staff investigators from the Commission on Quality of Care, I offered them rooms and assistance to help with their work. I reached out to shake hands, and one investigator was quick to say that he knows about me and was there to shut me down. He didn't want any handshake, but his supervisor promptly came over to correct him and thank us for the offer of help.

After working for more than 50 years in jails and prisons, they held the presumption that I was connected to the "wrong people," part of a criminal-type network. Maybe they thought that after my years of working with criminals, I could possibly provide evidence that might lead to convictions.

Statistics from a New York State survey indicated that people who transitioned into our agency aftercare programs successfully reintegrated into the community more than 90% of the time. Our record of providing successful re-entry for over 40,000 inmates in the ASAT programs was also a source of pride. As founder of these programs, it was difficult to have lost the capacity to provide aftercare treatment, housing and jobs for people expecting our help. We lost our open door and the investigations prevented any "supply to meet the need" for our many statewide programs.

For many years, investigators tracked my emails and telephone calls, sharing them with the media. This has continued to create negative ideas about our ministry.

Some guilty people were caught and then told to stay inside the agency to gather documentation without us knowing it. Perhaps that would uncover evidence they could use in plea bargains. One day at the Capitol, some reporters were eager to tell me how they knew about the informants. One shared what he knew about a sealed conviction held in an Albany County Court. The person in question had been working with us for years in an effort to gather information and gain his freedom, yet proven guilty by the state's investigation. Soon I found out that there were people who had agreed to be informants for the prosecution in exchange for not going to prison.

Reflections

Now 90 years old and dealing with a series of health difficulties, the word "retirement" comes up with most of my friends and visitors. I had to resign from church duties at age 75, but carried on much of my ministry with the freedom to prioritize how to best fulfill a lifelong desire to use the ability I have to "see the need and attempt to help."

Priesthood was a gift and attempting to help was easy at St. John's with over a hundred people walking in everyday seeking solutions to resolve their current crisis. I had networking skills and could guide them to agencies with the resources to assist them.

As a member of the clergy, whenever I called a politician or agency, they would take time to listen. The poor would not be able to enjoy the "listening ear" that I had as a pastor. My alliance with the needy gave them the ability to get respect from "power people" and opened doors to possible solutions.

The South End experience afforded me the opportunity to live and work with these good people as friends and neighbors, showing them a path to trust in our efforts to help. While I responded in a traditional pastoral role, poverty conditions became a challenge for social services, something I had become knowledgeable about. I attempted to expand their outlook into statewide brainstorming to develop systemic changes to help the needy. One of the priorities I was quick to embrace was helping the addicted and the homeless obtain the dignity of a paycheck.

A few people have learned that I was blessed with money from my family's investments. I could have chosen a relaxed type of lifestyle, but the challenge to be an agent of change, put to me by my Navy captain, set me on a path to a very happy life. From my high school days to my eighty-ninth year, my journey has been blessed with good health and willing people to assist in the cause of helping others in need.

For me, it was important to be an instrument of change but not be celebrated for any positive results. Whatever happened to the spirit of young people coming out of school with high ideals of giving back? Now everyone seems to stress more self-serving goals rather than those of helping others. The "me" factor appears to be ascendant.

My education stressed "giving and not receiving," and as I look back, I am happy with what life has had to offer. It is God and not me. I just followed the vocation that was the call for my agenda and what I was allowed to accomplish. Whatever sacrifices were made were never difficult.

Looking back at people who have been able to find a better life has been my joy. I quietly sit back and listen to some of the stories of clients who have come into our programs and who I now call "wounded healers." I listen to those who tell me daily how our programs have given them the freedom of a better life. It has been exciting to know clients who took advantage of the opportunities that were offered. As they tell their success stories, others in the group listen and have hope that "if that person can do it, so can I." The motivation inspires them to fight and hang on until the miracle happens.

From my 1959 appointment as a visitor to the state hospital, I witnessed the tragic lifestyle of people who were suffering with either mental or physical disabilities. My challenge was to use the gift of good health and recruit many of my friends in an attempt to improve their opportunities.

I know that the prayer of "serenity" has been my philosophy. Books have been written about how this prayer can change lives, but it has to be with God's help. We usually say the prayer at the end of every group session and hope that those in the room will sincerely try "just one more day" to work hard and to become the better person that God can help them to be… and to be patient, and "wait for the miracle to happen."

It will happen, be assured of that! Faith is the fourth leg of the stool. For myself I pray that God will continue to allow me to enjoy good health to keep the dream alive for those who need help. It is in the fifth chapter of Matthew, the beatitudes, where we are called to assist those in need. If we are not part of the solution, then we are part of the problem.

When we first started doing this work with the homeless, addicted and needy, we put together our own team. Most of it was based on experience or simply a desire to serve, to do something for folks in need. Nobody was certified, experience was gained on the job, most were volunteers and those who did get paid most certainly were not about to get rich. The job was done, the folks were fed, housed and medical needs were seen to. Employment opportunities were explored and jobs obtained. Everyone worked together for the joy of being able to help people, and the folks that were helped felt that they had the personal interest of our staff.

Things began to change around the mid-1970s. Suddenly, the certified professionals from other agencies and the state were upon us because they had discovered there was money to be made. If the new federal social service laws were applied, the agencies and the state would get a certain percentage for every individual helped. Of course, they would not be paid unless the "helpers" were certified and had been properly credentialed by the federal bureaucracy.

We found ourselves pushed aside and told we could no longer assist because we were not properly certified. Because alcohol and substance abuse counseling was so new, there were no certification standards in place yet. I was allowed to continue my role from a desk in the baptistery of St. John's Church. The rest of my staff was told to go home, obtain the required training, and then they would again be permitted to assist people.

Along with all of the certification came vast quantities of paperwork and forms for clients to fill out. The personal experience was lost and it has never come back. This is sad because people have become just another case number whose paperwork must be completed before any assistance can be given.

The face of social services has become a wall over which those in need must crawl. As a result, many of them do not get served and fall between the cracks. Thus begins the cycle of desperation. The personal atmosphere and concern of earlier years is gone—it's all about the paperwork. If somewhere along the line someone is helped, fine, but be sure the paperwork is properly completed, one way or another.

The tail seems to be wagging the dog. I understand that because of the money and multiple levels of government involved, things had to change. But I miss the days when we got to know all of our clients personally and were able to make things happen in a special and personal way.

I thought back to my days in school, studying supply-and-demand economics, as I tried to evaluate and identify opportunities that would save the taxpayers money and, at the same time, offer our inmate constituents the dignity of a paycheck.

As I grow older, I think about how lucky I've been. I rethink with gratitude some of the grace from God that I have received. I know some might ridicule me for some of my beliefs, but my thinking in life has always been that God can inspire people to be in the right place at the right time to make changes for others—just as I prayed about my reasons for going into the priesthood.

Pass It On

A popular 12-step slogan says, "Pass it On." It's attributed to the co-founder of Alcoholics Anonymous, Bill Wilson. His journey of addiction leading to recovery was a long and arduous one. After several failed attempts at sobriety, he experienced a spiritual conversion and a friend with whom he shared this experience persuaded him to turn himself over to the care of a higher power.

Bill surrendered himself amid cries of despair. Afterward, he experienced a new serenity. He never drank again for the remainder of his life. He joined an evangelical Christian group and tried to help other alcoholics, but succeeded only in keeping sober himself.

During a failed business trip, Bill was tempted to drink again and decided that to remain sober he needed to help another alcoholic. He called phone numbers in a church directory and eventually secured an introduction to Dr. Bob Smith, an alcoholic and a member of the same evangelical group as Bill. Together they began working with other alcoholics, sharing their pain and struggles as well as their experience, strength and hope. Thus began the fellowship that eventually became known as Alcoholics Anonymous.

As I shared earlier, I first began the mission of working with sick and suffering addicts during my assignment at St. John's Parish in the inner city of Albany. I did so with the help of others who saw the need and responded with generous hearts. Those we helped in turn responded to give back to other addicts by sharing their experience, strength and hope. I have always called them "wounded healers," where each one can teach another and pass on the gift of recovery.

For 61 years, I have witnessed this journey of receiving and giving. I have felt blessed to work side-by-side with thousands of our wounded healers, our dedicated and selfless staff, and those in public service who embraced our mission and supported us in so many ways. And I am most grateful to the wonderful donors who have supported us with their treasure. This generosity enables us to carry on with the mission of offering the three-legged stool of treatment, housing and industries, empowering our clients to reach the "Glidepath to Recovery."

Now I find myself in the twilight of my life, diagnosed with Stage 4 metastatic melanoma cancer. This has afforded me some extra time for reflection.

I feel a very deep gratitude for all that this journey has unfolded and blessed me with. I pray that the mission we began over 50 years ago will continue into the future and that all of us will work together to PASS IT ON…

God Bless,
Father Young

Unless someone offers a friendly smile,
a helping hand, a caring word, a listening ear,
somebody somewhere loses the courage to live…

EPILOGUE

On September 9, 2020, Father Young received a medical report that set the course for the last chapter of his life's journey. On that same day, he sat at the entrance to the annual Peter G. Young Foundation Gala at Saratoga National Golf Club, greeting and laughing with every one of the over 300 guests, friends and foundation employees in attendance, many of whom had supported his mission for over 50 years.

This was his final "thank you," his last gift to everyone present. He charmed people with his laughter and humor, recalling old stories, good and bad—not once speaking of his diagnosis. The handshakes and hugs were firmer and lasted longer than in the past. For most of those he encountered, this was goodbye, although his guests did not know it. Finally, on December 9, 2020, he left us knowing that his life's mission was complete.

And it was complete. Father Young left an established network in the hands of people he had guided, led, instructed and, in many cases, treated, so they could carry on his life's work. He created four separate organizations: a treatment provider, a housing program, a training program and a fundraising arm. Father Young devoted his life to serving his parishioners as well as the addicted, people in prison and others all-too-often considered unworthy of attention, let alone support.

Father Young leaves behind a solid structure, a mechanism to deliver on his mission. It has survived him, and it is thriving. Today, the programs are predominately located in the Capital Region of New York State, with tentacles reaching out to western New York, the Southern Tier and the Adirondacks. His programs serve over 2,000 clients per day providing treatment, housing and jobs.

The many thousands whose lives have been changed by Father Young are a living testament to his mission as they grow and thrive.

Although Father Young's earthly journey has come to a close, his legacy endures. And Father Young's mission continues.

Kevin A. Luibrand
PYHIT Board President

PYHIT TODAY

Peter Young Housing, Industries and Treatment (PYHIT) provides treatment, housing and jobs to those suffering alcohol and drug addictions. These services are the basis of Father Young's three-legged stool strategy of support.

PYHIT includes four nonprofits—all 501(c)(3) organizations:

- 820 River Street, Inc. – Provides recovery and support services through the individual's recovery process.
- The Altamont Program, Inc. – Provides multiple levels of residential housing from supportive living to independent living.
- Vesta Community Housing Development Board, Inc. – Owns 12 properties from which the PYHIT services are provided.
- The Father Peter G. Young, Jr. Foundation Inc. – Provides fundraising and communications services.

Collectively, these organizations provide the rehabilitation and housing services that Father Young has successfully provided for over 50 years.

The Board of PYHIT has made a commitment to its clients, staff, and supporters that Father Young's journey of compassion for the socially disenfranchised will continue, uninterrupted. While they miss Father's leadership and encouragement, they will honor his memory and legacy by continuing to work hard every day to support those in need of PYHIT services.

Here is a summary of the programs and services provided in 2022:

Outpatient Clinics

Eleanor Young Outpatient Clinic | Albany, NY
Father Young's first facility started in 1969 providing:
- Honor Court; DWI Program
- CRPA (Certified Recovery Peer Advocate) Certification
- Medicated Assisted Treatment Services
- 12-Step Recovery Groups

Baywood Clinic | Queensbury, NY
- ABLE (Alternative to a Better Living Environment) - Transition Coordinator in County Jails
- Wellness Program-YMCA; Community Outreach Services; DWI Program
- CRPA (Certified Recovery Peer Advocate) University; School-based counseling
- Warren County Dept. of Soc. Services: providing counseling and evaluation services
- Medicated Assisted Treatment Services; 12-Step Recovery Groups

Family Shelter
- Schuyler Inn, Menands, NY - with 110 rooms, it's the largest family shelter in Albany County, assisting both families and single adults during the COVID Pandemic.
- Other Programs provided at the Schuyler Inn include:
  - Home Meal Delivery: delivering over 57,000 meals annually mostly in rural Albany County
  - South-end Pantry Food distribution
  - Alliance for Better Health Partner (Food is Medicine)
  - Services Vocational Education: Contracted by Albany County
  - Established with Albany County support, new training methods for employment skills development using tele-training

Men's Shelter
- Schenectady Monastery – Shelter has 36 housing units and 14 single residence occupancy units
- Contracted COVID quarantine beds totaling 2,555 bed nights for the year, plus providing Code Blue beds in Schenectady

Women's Shelter
- Troy, NY – 14 housing units, with various support services

Supportive and Transitional Housing
- Albany, NY – 59 housing units in 8 locations
- Glens Falls, NY – 20 housing units in a single location

Veteran's Housing
- Syracuse, NY – In the Spring 2022, the Altamont Program was awarded a VA Capital Grant to purchase a 79-room hotel to operate a Veterans Residential Program.
- Buffalo, NY – 34 bed Shelter Program providing Residential Case Management including re-entry into community living.

APPRECIATION AND ACKNOWLEDGMENTS

Jackie Gentile
Jackie was with PYHIT from 1986 to 2016, served as Chief Operating Officer from 1990 through 2016, and assisted Father Young in many aspects of his life's journey. She also provided invaluable assistance to Father Young in the organization and editing of this manuscript.

Dr. Laetitia Rhatigan, STD
Laetitia worked with Father Young beginning in 1969 as the first secretary of the Albany Council on Alcoholism. She was a staff member and Director of Faith Formation from 1976–1983 at Blessed Sacrament Parish, Bolton Landing, NY. And she was privileged to assist Father in the preparation of his autobiography.

Billy Balfe
Billy, Director of Housing for PYHIT, was Father Young's cousin and was always available to support Father's healthcare needs during the last years of his journey.

Kevin Luibrand
Kevin serves as President of the Board of Father Young's nonprofit organizations. As an attorney, he has worked tirelessly as a volunteer

providing legal services to Father Young's organizations and also defending many individuals in Father Young's programs.

The PYHIT Board Members

Since the inception of PYHIT in 1985, all board members have served as unpaid volunteers in support of Father's Young's programs.

PYHIT Past CEOs

After Father Young's retirement in 2011, several unpaid volunteer CEOs stepped up to fulfill his leadership role: Martin Cirrincione (2011–2014), Robert McMahon (2014–2017) and Peter Newkirk (2017–2022).

Stephen Dzinanka, Digital XPress

Steve edited Father Young's manuscript and was invaluable in directing the layout and organization of this autobiography.

Designed by **Michele Wyse, Digital XPress.**

Printed by **Digital XPress**, Albany, NY.